Advance Praise for
The Spirit of ACE: Celebrating 15 Years

"For fifteen years, teachers in the Alliance for Catholic Education (ACE) have blessed our nation's Catholic schools with their service, commitment, and dedication. With deep care and concern for their students, the communities in which they live and serve, and their own development as teachers of faith, they are a source of light, energy, and hope to the lives they touch. *The Spirit of ACE: Celebrating 15 Years* provides a glimpse into the grace-filled days of the lives of these ACE teachers. Moments of joy, challenge, and witness are contained in these pages and this collection will stand as an inspiration for all of us who are committed to Catholic schooling in the United States."

Rev. John I. Jenkins, C.S.C.
President, University of Notre Dame

The Spirit of ACE: Celebrating 15 Years

THE SPIRITUAL AND PASTORAL TEXTS AND RESOURCES DIVISION

Alliance for Catholic Education Press
at the University of Notre Dame

The *Spirit* of ACE:
Celebrating 15 Years

Edited by
Laura Budzichowski
Zack Budzichowski
Tony DeSapio
K.C. Kenney
Kathy Steinlage

ALLIANCE FOR CATHOLIC EDUCATION PRESS
AT THE UNIVERSITY OF NOTRE DAME

NOTRE DAME, INDIANA

Copyright © 2008

Alliance for Catholic Education Press
at the University of Notre Dame
158 I.E.I. Building
Notre Dame, IN 46556
http://www.nd.edu/~acepress

All rights reserved.

Text design by Julie Wernick Dallavis
Cover design by Mary Jo Adams Kocovski

ISBN 978-0-9788793-4-1

Scripture texts in this work are taken from the *New American Bible with Revised New Testament and Revised Psalms* © 1991, 1986, 1970 Confraternity of Christian Doctrine, Washington, D.C. and are used by permission of the copyright owner. All Rights Reserved. No part of the *New American Bible* may be reproduced in any form without permission in writing from the copyright owner.

"Cross Country Czar" by William Priestley reprinted from *25 in Mississippi* © 2008 William M. Priestley and used with permission of the copyright owner. http://www.lulu.com/content/2178196

"Prophets of a Future Not Our Own" by Kenneth Untener reprinted with permission of Auxiliary Bishop Emeritus Thomas Gumbleton of the Archdiocese of Detroit.

Library of Congress Cataloging-in-Publication Data

The spirit of ACE : celebrating 15 years / edited by Laura Budzichowski. ... [et al.].
   p. cm.
   ISBN 978-0-9788793-4-1 (pbk. : alk. paper)
   1. Alliance for Catholic Education (University of Notre Dame) 2. Catholic Church--Education--United States. 3. Catholic teachers--United States. I. Budzichowski, Laura, 1974- II. Alliance for Catholic Education (University of Notre Dame)

   LC501.S65 2008
   371.071'273--dc22
                        2008021033

This book was printed on acid-free paper.
Printed in the United States of America

Contents

Acknowledgments   *xi*

Introduction

Introduction
   Tim Scully, C.S.C.   1
Looking Back and Moving Forward:
ACE and the Sustaining Power of Memory
   John J. Staud   5

Teaching

Journeys to Discovery
   Blaine C. Ackley   11
Teaching: A Strange Calling
   Tom "Doc" Doyle   13
Between Mississippi and South Bend
   Laura Eidietis, ACE 4 Biloxi   17
Mr. Healey's Inferno
   Matthew S. Healey, ACE 2 Biloxi   19
Refined Elegance
   Kate Sullivan, ACE 8 Jackson   23
Gratitude
   K.C. Kenney, ACE 12 Mobile   25
Eight Hundred Sets of Eyes
   Katelyn Rosa, ACE 6 Brownsville   29
Cross Country Czar
   William Priestley, ACE 12 Biloxi   31
Precipitation
   Marshall Davidson, ACE 12 Los Angeles   33
The Virtue of Humility
   Kelly (Perry) Buyske, ACE 9 Tucson   35
The Greatest Teacher
   Tom Jacobs, ACE 2 Oklahoma City   37
Never Give Up
   Dominic Yonto, ACE 12 St. Petersburg   41
The Motivation Debate
   Michael Macaluso, ACE 11 Baton Rouge   43

To the Death
    Mariaelena (Raymond) Amato, ACE 7 Los Angeles   47
Miracle on San Felipe Street
    Laura Aull, ACE 10 San Antonio   49
Answered Prayer
    Francisco Ramirez, ACE 11 Kansas City   51
Teaching: The Art of Persuasion
    Fr. Ronald Nuzzi, ACE Leadership Director   53
Roots of Identity
    Maria Loebig-Haberle, ACE 6 Nashville   57
The Annex
    Antonio Ortiz, ACE 5 Mission   59
A Lesson in Church Hierarchy
    Johnnie Quigley, ACE 14 Dallas   63
Year of the Ducks
    Amy Vanden Boogart, ACE 11 Kansas City   65
Sam's Life Lessons
    Walter Pruchnik, ACE 12 St. Petersburg   67
The Courage to Dream
    Beau Schweitzer, ACE 7 Los Angeles   69
The Perfect Season
    John Bacsik, ACE 11 Savannah   73
Basketweaver
    Emmeline Schoen D'Agostino, ACE 10 Tucson   75
The Price of Honesty
    Justin Meyers, ACE 10 Pensacola   79

Community

Blessed, Broken, and Shared: Communities of Hope
    Sean McGraw, C.S.C.   83
What Remains
    Dave Devine, ACE 1 Baton Rouge   87
Chicken Italiano
    Molly (Davis) Hahn, ACE 3 Tulsa   91
We Can Do That
    Michael Faggella-Luby, ACE 5 Jacksonville   93
The Room That Boxes Built
    Eric Amato, ACE 8 Los Angeles   97
Running on Empty
    Michael Downs, ACE 7 Austin   99

Oh, the Places You'll Go!
    Phil Autrey, ACE 2 Charlotte   103

The Thursday of The Beast
    Colleen Moak Ringa, ACE 9 Austin   107

Car Troubles
    Heidi Eppich Druist, ACE 7 Tulsa   109

My Own Mission in Education
    Scott Reis, ACE 5 Charlotte   111

My Shield, My Spear, and My Armor
    Araceli Ramirez, ACE 7 Austin   115

Mathematics of Friendship
    Elizabeth Stowe, ACE 12 Biloxi   117

Why Don't They Come Live With Us?
    Jen (Mullins) Podichetty, ACE 5 Corpus Christi   119

The "Pillar" of Community
    Beth A. Burau, ACE 7 Dallas   123

Oh, Christmas Tree
    Thomas Perez, ACE 2 Savannah   127

MemphACE Memories
    Dave Archibald, ACE 10 Memphis   129

My Running Angel
    Tiffany Roman, ACE 9 Dallas   131

The Community of Holy Rosary
    Tricia Sevilla, ACE 6 Jacksonville, ACE Leadership 6   133

Love Letters from Southeast L.A.
    Clare Bush, ACE 12 Los Angeles   137

Community is a Texas Marathon
    Sarah Bates, ACE 12 Denver   139

I Had Every Reason to Stay Home
    Tony Hollowell, ACE 11 Biloxi   143

Spirituality

Tears to Joy: Daring to Race with the Winds of the Spirit
    Lou DelFra, C.S.C.   149

We Cannot Do Everything
    John Daily, ACE 7 Mission   155

The ACE American Fellowship Tour: A Closer Look
    Karl Franz Flasch Hendrickson, ACE 11 Mobile   159

My ACE Mission
    Laura Cunniff, ACE 12 Mission   163

The Privileged Work of the Holy Spirit
    Ted Lefere, ACE 4 Biloxi   165
An ACE Parable
    Keiran Roche, ACE 13 Mobile   167
Rejection, Then Acceptance
    Eric T. Pernotto, ACE 10 Brownsville   169
Encountering God in Failure
    Tisha (Greenslade) Frost, ACE 8 Baton Rouge   173
Idealist Without Illusions
    Michael J. Werner, ACE 8 Tucson   177
Lenten Reconciliation
    Kevin Somok, ACE 11 Austin   179
Silhouettes
    Kevin Burke, ACE 9 Phoenix   183
A Rambling Answer to a Short Question
    Patrick O'Sullivan, ACE 2 Charleston   185
Please, Lord: A Soldier's Experience of Grace
    Ryan P. Hinton, ACE 11 Savannah   189
Don't Stop Believing: The Journey of an ACE 11
    Laura Giannuzzi, ACE 11 Pensacola   193
How I Became a Principal
    Tricia Sevilla, ACE 6 Jacksonville, ACE Leadership 6   197
This is Not What I Signed Up For
    Nick Huck, ACE 11 Atlanta   201

Appendix

Cast Your Nets Deeper: Celebrating 10 Years of ACE
    Tim Scully, C.S.C.   207
ACE Facts   217

About the Editors   219

Acknowledgments

Many thanks to the following people that helped make this book possible:

ACE Senior Leadership Team
ACE Press
Laura Aull
Ricky Austin
Kevin Burke
Clare Bush
Steve Camilleri
Emmeline D'Agostino
Julie Dallavis
Tim Green
George Keegan
MJ Adams Kocovski
Joe Hettler
Molly Kahn
Marisa Limon
Chelsea Madison
Brian Moscona
Fr. Ronald Nuzzi
Jeni Rinner
Lou Weber

Introduction
Tim Scully, C.S.C.
Co-Founder
Chairman of the Executive Committee
Alliance for Catholic Education

Fr. Scully, together with Fr. Sean McGraw, co-founded the ACE program in 1993. With Scully's vision and commitment, in just fifteen years, ACE's reach and influence have extended far beyond the forty ACE 1 teachers sent to serve in eight dioceses. Scully was instrumental in bringing about the formation of the University Consortium for Catholic Education (UCCE), a partnership between the University of Notre Dame and fourteen other colleges and universities interested in building on ACE's successful model to start or strengthen their own teacher service programs. Collectively, the fifteen programs place over four hundred teachers per year in under-resourced Catholic and parochial schools. Scully is currently a professor of Political Science at the University of Notre Dame, a fellow of the Helen Kellogg Institute for International Studies, and serves as Director of Notre Dame's Institute for Educational Initiatives, where he oversees ACE's continuing mission as well as work done by the Center for Research on Educational Opportunity and other education-related programs.

It was a beautiful spring evening, fifteen years ago, in Berkeley. I was on sabbatical, trying to write my new book on political parties, but I was admittedly distracted. By 8:00 p.m. California time, my distraction had devolved into a full-blown panic. I had been calling Sean McGraw, who was back at Notre Dame, hourly, inquiring as to how many applications had arrived for a new program we were trying to start. The news was grim. Sean had placed an empty box carton outside my office in the Hesburgh Center, but it was still practically empty as of late afternoon on the day of the deadline. Dribs and drabs. I'd make a final call, I decided. I feared the worst, for the deadline had just come and gone.

I held my breath, and called. Sean picked up the phone. He was roaring with laughter. "Tim, you wouldn't believe this! We had five applications about ten minutes ago, but literally in the last five minutes, ninety applications just came showering in! We are swimming in applications for this thing!" Notre Dame's seniors, our very first members of ACE, had responded to our invitation in numbers we had never dared to dream and on a time schedule we would soon get used to!

Of course, our elation was short-lived. We began to read the applications and reality slowly sank in. We had recruited these awesomely talented and generous candidates for teaching jobs that we didn't quite yet have; and for a Master's Degree in Teaching which didn't quite yet exist; to live in community houses that we hadn't quite yet located. Yikes!

We have sometimes referred to the beginnings of ACE fifteen years ago as a story of improvising on Providence. And we do so because as an ACE community, we have truly experienced, over the course of the past fifteen years, the most amazing and surprising moments of unexpected grace, together. From the (mostly self-proclaimed!) "heroic" days of ACE 1, through the pioneering initial years, to the tenth anniversary celebrations where we proclaimed our intent to "Cast Our Nets Deeper," we have tried to listen carefully to the stirrings of the Holy Spirit in our midst. And, holy smokes, has the Holy Spirit ever responded! She's been "bouncin' off the walls!"

In its brief fifteen-year history, ACE has become the nation's premier provider of talent and expertise to Catholic schools. Over a thousand faith-filled and passionate women and men have taken up the challenge, joining our mission in service to the children and young people in America's underserved classrooms. We have recently undertaken to meet the critical leadership needs of our schools, with dozens and dozens of candidates in our signature Master's Degree in Educational Administration with an exclusive focus on Catholic educational leadership. We have formed the beginnings of a national apostolic movement in the ACE Fellowship, with an aim to provide new hope and life to our faith tradition. We have initiated a novel English-as-a-New-Language licensing effort for those who serve the growing numbers of school children of immigrant communities, a central thrust of our educational mission.

And there's still more. We have created innovative partnerships with at-risk Catholic schools in our nation's inner cities—our Magnificat Schools. Through grace and grit, and with the help of the ACE community and Fellowship nationally, we are beginning to see these schools transfigure into beacons of hope in crumbling neighborhoods. We have built ACE Consulting nationwide to strengthen the institutional viability of our most fragile schools. We have launched a national initiative, together with partners at the NCEA and the United States Department of Education, to more effectively capture and utilize the resources legally due faith-based schools from the public purse.

We have laid the foundations for a new national focus for research on Catholic schools at Notre Dame, and have identified the resources to invite scholars and graduate fellows to undertake the urgent task of re-articulating the case for what sociologist James Coleman previously called "the Catholic school advantage." We have incubated the nation's only national academic journal focusing on themes related to Catholic education, and we have launched our own ACE Press. Among ourselves, we know that the Catholic school experience is valuable, but we need rigorous empirical research to demonstrate it in today's culture and context. And we intend to produce just that.

Notre Dame's ACE cannot and will not travel this journey in service to the urgent needs of America's Catholic schools alone. So, we have joined forces with fourteen other Catholic colleges and universities and formed a national alliance to sustain and strengthen Catholic schools, our great "national treasures," as Secretary of Education Margaret Spellings so vividly called them several months ago on our campus. Gathering recently at the Carnegie Foundation, a number of America's leading Catholic colleges and universities forged a novel partnership to focus our resources collectively to serve the urgent needs of our at-risk Catholic schools. We will not be deterred.

What a journey we have had these past fifteen years, since that shower of applications introduced us to the first ACE teachers! I love to remember that moment of reading those first files, and meeting those first teachers. Of all our many "beginnings" in ACE, this is the most important, the most delightful, the most full of grace. Because, when I look back over the past decade and a half, the gift for which I am most grateful, the most lasting and lovely fruit the Spirit has given us are the people—the ACErs—the individual, and now collective (and in increasing numbers marital!) vocation stories, that make up the life spirit of ACE. The stories that have been collected in this book of essays are a prodigious testament to the ongoing presence of that Life and Spirit. Thanks be to God!

Looking Back and Moving Forward: ACE and the Sustaining Power of Memory

John J. Staud
Senior Director, Pastoral Formation and Administration
Alliance for Catholic Education

Dr. Staud joined the ACE program in 1996 as Associate Director, later moving into the role of Director of ACE before taking the title of Director of Pastoral Formation and Administration in 2000. Staud has been a strong advocate of Catholic schools, not only through his enthusiastic recruitment, placement, and support of ACE teachers, but also as a Fellow with the Institute of Educational Initiatives, where he served as a principal author and editor of the final report of the Notre Dame Task Force on Catholic Education. Staud and his wife have three children, all of whom attend Christ the King Catholic School in South Bend, Indiana, where he serves on the School Board. Prior to joining ACE, Staud taught British and American literature at Loyola University of Chicago and at Jesuit high schools in Chicago and Denver.

"It's actually hard to remember what life was like before ACE."

These words, spoken by MJ Adams Kocovski a few years ago during a reflection on a staff retreat, have stayed with me, and not just because I find them to be strangely reassuring when I experience the memory losses of encroaching middle age. For MJ's point, one that resonated with so many of us on the ACE staff that autumn afternoon, testifies more to the power of memories formed in ACE than to forgetfulness about life before ACE. For me, those memories began to accumulate from my first encounters with the generous, enthusiastic, and faith-filled people who make the program what it is.

I'll never forget my first ACE Mass, in particular my first ACE sign of peace. My wife, Jenny, and I had come to town in June 1996 to look for a house, and we attended the Sunday night Mass in Keenan-Stanford chapel, back when ACE was not so large as to require the Basilica. At the sign of peace, I gave my bride a delicate kiss, shook the hand of a silver-haired person to my right, and turned around to find myself drawn into the full embrace of a towering figure, my face pressed uncomfortably into his sternum. "Welcome to ACE!" said the six-foot, seven-inch Dan McGinty as he released me with a broad grin. Dan's hospitality had left me rather shaken, and my face must have registered the shock. Surveying the enthusiastic outbreak of hugs in the chapel, Jenny leaned over to me and laughed: "Looking around here, I think this may be part of your job description."

As it turns out, no job description could ultimately capture the all-encompassing intensity of the ACE experience, for participants and staff alike. I chuckle at the memory of Dan's startling welcome, which I have come to see as embodying the spirit of hospitality and joy that animates ACE. This memory of my welcome to ACE also reminds me how much my association with the multitude of people in our "alliance"—colleagues, graduates, diocesan administrators, and especially participants—has enriched my life and deepened my faith in Christ, who, after all, came to earth as a teacher.

What drew me to ACE in the first place was the opportunity to return to my alma mater to work with a new program that sought to make a difference for Catholic schools, truly one of my life's passions and one I inherit directly from my mother and father, who made Catholic education the center of life for our family. What keeps me engaged is a complex mixture of anxiety and hope.

I do worry about the future of Catholic schools because they are under duress and because I am convinced that they represent the most important mission of the Church in the United States. Imagine the Church in America without them. To quote the report of the Notre Dame Task Force on Catholic Education: "Would it be as robust and vital? How would it produce generous leaders? How would it serve immigrants? How would it provide avenues of educational opportunity to the poor, especially those in our cities?" We confront powerful threats and believe that our future depends greatly on the vitality of our Catholic schools. Selfishly, perhaps, I want them to be strong for my grandchildren and their children, too, for I love these schools and the people who commit their lives to them.

At the same time, I see remarkable signs of hope. Work on the Task Force project with Tim Scully and others helped me to see that although enrollments may be half of what they were in the year of my birth, the fact that our nation's

Catholic schools remain the largest system of private schools in the world in the midst of sweeping cultural, demographic, and financial change is indeed reason for hope. More positively, we sense an increasing urgency among many Catholics and those who may worship outside our faith tradition to preserve these "national treasures" and we see new initiatives across the land to accomplish this goal.

In his introduction, Tim charts the providential growth of ACE. We have come a long way in fifteen years, and programmatic growth and continual improvement have become ingrained expectations for all of us. Is it fair to say that ACE represents one of the most important signs of hope for Catholic schools and for the broader Church in the United States? Certainly many outside Notre Dame have made that claim. Our central challenge, then, is to summon the courage and imagination to see ourselves as others see us—as, for example, the late John Cardinal O'Connor saw ACE after presiding at the summer Missioning Mass when he told Tim that ACE was not a program so much as an apostolic movement in service to Catholic schools. It can be at once humbling and energizing as we come to realize, increasingly over time, the extent of the invitation to discipleship we all share.

This invitation to discipleship lies at the heart of ACE, crucial to all we do. For no matter how many new initiatives arise at Notre Dame to respond to the needs of fragile Catholic elementary and secondary schools, we know that ACE will always be grounded in the recruitment and formation of talented men and women in service to those schools. "Always Changing Everything," you say? Absolutely! Still, over the years there has been one constant for me: a profound sense of humble gratitude at the generosity of those who have served in ACE. From interviews where people openly discuss those who have been their spiritual role models to difficult community meetings on site visits and retreats where we pray for grace to break into our lives—often at times of seeming impasse!—to summer Masses where my children have the privilege of experiencing a sense of the Church that will create, Jenny and I believe, sustaining memories for their lives of faith, I am repeatedly reminded that I am blessed beyond measure by the ACE community of faith, hope, and love. In the end, I stand as proof that even a man from Pittsburgh can learn to give an embrace, not only at the sign of peace but when ACE teachers and graduates return and walk through the doors of the Badin office. Now I do so with joy. So to all of you who have served in ACE, heartfelt thanks. You bring hope to the world. ✪

TEACHING

"When he saw the crowds, he went up the mountain, and after he had sat down, his disciples came to him. He began to teach them." (Matthew 5:1)

"There are different kinds of spiritual gifts but the same Spirit; there are different forms of service but the same Lord; there are different workings but the same God who produces all of them in everyone." (1 Corinthians 12:4-6)

Journeys to Discovery
Blaine C. Ackley
Associate Professor of Education
The University of Portland

Dr. Ackley was the Faculty Coordinator for The University of Portland Masters in Education Program that served the first four classes of ACE teachers. In addition to lending his many talents to launching the Master's component of the ACE program, his enthusiasm and professionalism in the classroom set a tremendous example for all who were fortunate enough to have had him as a professor. He has since helped to establish the Pacific Alliance for Catholic Education (PACE), which serves the needs of under-resourced Catholic schools in the Northwest and Pacific Rim. Ackley is currently a Fulbright Scholar-in-Residence at the School of Education in the Catholic University of Temuco, located in Temuco, Chile, through August 2008. His Fulbright position is to help English language teachers improve their instructional practices and to conduct research on teacher self-efficacy.

Any time a teacher can find a student, a group of students, or better yet, a whole class of students who are bright, curious, committed, and passionate about learning and life, it becomes a memorable moment of exhilaration. Such moments become sparks of memory in the synapses of our brains which evoke fond connections of camaraderie for all of the people who shared the experience. ACE was one of those experiences for me and I believe that all of us who shared the ACE experience can count ourselves as especially blessed to have shared those special moments of learning, joy, and camaraderie together.

I have always admired the early ACE groups as true pioneer adventurers. In many cases, they found that they had volunteered to teach an as-yet-undetermined class or subject at a school location that was not quite certain. These details would take care of themselves, but they learned to go with the flow, for it seemed the ACE acronym really stood for "Always Changing Everything." When I think about it now, I am sure that the early ACE teachers arrived at their classrooms with the complete set of the required teacher competencies of flexibility and responding to ambiguous situations.

Later, I had the pleasure of visiting with many of the communities and classrooms. Sean McGraw, Lou DelFra, Joe Pascarelli, and I were able to watch ACErs grow in professional roles as teachers and in personal roles as members of a community. I watched as they evolved from novice teachers who did not know many of the school protocols into competent, professional teaching peers. The success ACE has enjoyed is due in large measure to the success that ACE teachers had in the classroom and the divine inspiration we all had for our work.

Unlike many other professions, teachers enjoy the unique opportunity to touch the future as we work with our students. It is through ACE teachers' embodiment of Christ the Teacher that I have been able to touch the future as well. Let us continue our journey of discovery and learning by teaching and speaking out for justice, equality, freedom, and educational opportunity for everyone whenever and wherever our journeys may take us in the future.

May we all live in peace and harmony and may God bless all teachers and our sacred mission.

Teaching: A Strange Calling

Tom "Doc" Doyle
Senior Director, Academic Programs
Alliance for Catholic Education

Dr. Doyle joined the ACE program as an adjunct professor in 1996 and has served as the Academic Director since 2002—the latest endeavor in over thirty-five years of strengthening and supporting Catholic education. Following his graduation from Notre Dame with a Ph.D. in Physics, Doyle returned to the Archdiocese of Mobile, Alabama, and over the years has served as the Associate Superintendent, Federal Projects Director, and Acting Vicar for Education. He taught and served as Principal and President at Montgomery Catholic High School from 1972 until 2001. His lasting commitment to the Archdiocese of Mobile was most notably recognized when a middle school in Montgomery, Alabama was named in his honor—Thomas L. Doyle Middle School—where ACE teachers currently serve. Doyle brings a wealth of perspective and experience to his current position as Academic Director. In addition to his work with the Archdiocese of Mobile and ACE, Doyle has also served as Chair of the Alabama State Advisory Council and continues to serve on school boards and academic councils in many different capacities. His service to Catholic school teachers and administrators through workshops and presentations is invaluable.

Teaching is such a strange calling, a calling and a ministry in the eyes of the Church. In what other profession would the first measure of success be determined by the learning—or lack thereof—of giggly, wiggly children or of hormonally distracted adolescents? Yet, academically, that is the acid measure. On more than one occasion I have found myself mulling the words of a Leonard Bernstein song from the musical *Wonderful Town:* "Why, oh why, oh why, oh why did I ever leave" physics? For teaching! Invariably, the answer lies in stories, my own and those of others who teach, particularly in recent years the stories from ACE teachers.

My first experience of an ACE class ended on a note of despair. Our class met in O'Shaughnessy Hall, for five hours a day in a small room barely large enough for the thirty students in the room. Knowing only the time frame, I had planned a lot of group work. In tight quarters and with much accommodation and noise, we developed lessons, units, and the outlines of courses. The ACErs were energetic, engaged, and sharp. It was a wonderful first class—until the last day, a Friday from 2 to 4 p.m. They all came, they said, to hear the end of a story that I had begun the day before. We finished our work, I told the story, and as we got up to leave, a student announced that "all this planning stuff is nice, but I'm just going to wing it with my students." My first ACE class and I failed.

Fortunately, there have been offsetting successes in my teaching career. High school ACE teachers may remember the story of Brian, whose Air Force family transferred to Montgomery when he was a sophomore and who were to be there only one year. Brian was angry for the first three months because he had been torn from his friends at the previous high school and again angry for the last three months because he was forced once again to leave new friends. As a pattern of minor defiance developed in the fall and ordinary consequences proved ineffective, my practice of having students come in on Saturday for chores around the school became a ritual with Brian; we came to know each other well. When he finished the one or two hour chore and came to get me, I would—dramatically—put on my glasses to inspect the work, and while doing so talk to him.

"Why are you here, Brian?"

"What will you do next week to be more cooperative?"

"How can we help?"

He would mumble through some answers and off he would go. Yet, slowly, he made progress both in behavior and more notably in academics.

End of the story? Not quite! Perhaps fifteen years later I received a two page, single-spaced, typed letter from Brian. The gist was that he wanted me to know that he was the proud father of two young girls, both of whom were in Catholic school; he was President of the Parish Council and was in his second year of an MBA program at a Catholic college. He ended by saying that while he listened to me on those many Saturday mornings, he couldn't hear the message until later. More credit to him, than to me. But, still!

My own first memory of being formed by a teacher occurred in first grade with Sister Antonio, a much loved nun—by the parents—because she was clear about acceptable behavior and expected learning in her classroom. The learning was no problem; the behavior was a tiny problem. Coming from a family that was economically stressed, I had only a few things that were mine. I had just gotten a box of new crayons, the kind in the green and yellow box with every point sharp and the crayons brilliantly displayed in two rows. I had trouble coloring within the lines, and the sharp points were, to my mind, key to doing so. Just as we started to color, Sister came by and saw that the girl next to me had no crayons, and she asked me to share. I can't remember that I said "no," but I was clearly reluctant and did so in bad humor; that resulted in my detention during recess, alone in the room to fume, which Sister allowed for five or six minutes but then gently and firmly guided me to regret and contrition. The moral was that staying within the lines was not as important as sharing generously with others. Though I did not learn everything that I needed to know in first grade, that lesson of generosity from a first grade teacher did remain with me.

More recently, voices from my first years of teaching have called to share warm and charitable stories about the physics and calculus classes they endured while I groped my way toward becoming a competent teacher. By happenstance, all three are doctors, and their consistent theme was about the extraordinary demands that I placed upon them. My response was that my demands were minor in comparison to their demands on me: physics questions that I had never thought about, perspectives on calculus problems that were entirely different from mine, situations that they wanted me to explain that I had no clue how to approach, and topics that I had learned only superficially in my undergraduate courses. A good question might be: Who taught whom? I suppose that the moral of their reflections is that I was a good actor, a trait of which my former homeroom teacher from high school, Brother Thaddeus, would have been proud—he who deliberately stirred up that class just before I walked in by asking whether they were prepared for the (non-existent) test that he had seen me running off on the faculty room copier.

The stories of ACE teachers and their trials and triumphs have added to my lore of teaching: Lynne Ruozzi teaching a wonderfully structured math lesson in Lake Charles only to have one student at the end claim utter futility at understanding or Tony Hollowell reminding me that students must "experience the content" and kindly attributing the phrase to me, or watching Katie Laird in Phoenix speaking almost no English in her Spanish class and engaging every student with energy and good humor. I hope each of them and many others have experienced the joy of teaching in the measure that has been given to me by students, including

ACErs. Teaching is a strange calling, its rewards are mysterious, and its joys are profound perhaps because, at its Catholic best, teaching is a communication between souls. ✪

Between Mississippi and South Bend

Laura Eidietis ✡ ACE 4 Biloxi

As I sit in a lower Manhattan high school observing a very inexperienced student teacher carve learning out of chaotic teenage energy and hormones, Pascagoula, Mississippi, and the Golden Dome seem very, very far away. I'm not the same person I was then with almost a decade, a research degree, two academic jobs, and a marriage later. Or am I? Keep in mind that this question is asked despite the tears in my eyes when NPR reported the rebuilding of the Biloxi Bay Bridge.

My student teacher asks me about defining appropriate boundaries for relationships with students, and instead of quoting from the educational literature, I am back in a classroom that smelled of the living sea, when it didn't smell of the sewage treatment plant across the street, and talking to a young man about why it was not appropriate to tease a teacher in quite so familiar a way. I guess we do not completely forget our old selves, rather we recall them in a different way. I recall an excerpt from my final ACE essay:

> As a teacher, my day begins at 6 a.m., I am at school preparing for class by shortly after 7 a.m., I teach four preps (five classes), spend two "planning periods" calling parents, grading, and rescheduling rain-out soccer games. At 3 p.m., I organize retakes of tests, detentions, and sit down for a half-hour of tutoring. By 4 p.m., I am on the soccer field coaching for two hours. At this point, I drive home for dinner and any last minute planning or grading that simply cannot wait. Saturdays are spent actually attempting the normal chores and errands necessary for life. Sundays are

spent grading and planning the next week. This schedule allows for almost no time for such activities as reflecting on teaching or developing year-long strategies.

I remember this. I remember it every time my inservice teachers, who are also my full-time students, tell me that he or she will be just a bit late on this or that assignment. I also remember this when my students become just a bit too focused on the mechanics of teaching and forget to reflect on who they are or what their purpose is as educators. One of my biggest challenges as a teacher educator has been challenging students to recognize that teaching is a vocation and civic responsibility. Oh, so much more than a job!

I also revisit this excerpt from my teaching philosophy that Dr. Maria made us write:

> My students in school will someday be students who have left school. Thus, I must help prepare students for their role in a society much larger than their school community. Most students are best prepared for the "outside world" by being taught to think as critically as possible and to communicate as clearly as possible. It is my responsibility to help my students understand how their intellectual skills can be used to fulfill their role in the world. Thus, I should make the subject matter of learning as relevant as possible.

In that essay, I was envisioning my teenagers, instead of my current twenty- to fifty-year-old undergraduates and graduate pre-service teachers. No matter, this is my philosophy. In fact, that first essay has been the basis of every teaching philosophy I have written since ACE. Thank goodness I had the draft already written almost a decade ago, somewhere between Mississippi and South Bend.

Mr. Healey's Inferno

Matthew S. Healey ⬤ ACE 2 Biloxi

The young teacher stood outside his door, greeting the children as they entered. Seventh graders piped, "Hello," and scuttled into the classroom. Today was Thursday—skit day—and the students bristled with excitement. The teacher smiled with self-satisfaction. And why shouldn't he? The skits had been a tremendous success in his classroom. Kids became excited about learning their vocabulary words, and test scores rose dramatically. Here, in this teacher's classroom, was proof that hands-on learning worked. His chest swelled with pride. "I am a teacher," he whispered to himself, "and life is good." Forgetting the proverb that "pride goeth before the fall," the naïve pedagogue entered his classroom, little knowing that he was stumbling into Hell.

The cow-eyed, eager girl had asked him on Monday if she could bring her cocker spaniel puppy in for her group's skit.

"Of course," the teacher responded confidently. Hearing this affirmative response, another young lady shrieked with delight.

"Can I bring my dog?" she asked, bursting out of her seat.

"Well, what kind is it?" asked the teacher, a note of hesitation in his voice. It was a black lab, full grown.

"Um, I babysit this little kid. Can I bring him? He would be perfect for our skit," came a voice from the back.

"Fine, fine," answered the teacher. "Let's just start writing the skits. We'll worry about the details later."

That had been Monday. And today was Thursday. Skit day. The students filed in. Gabrielle staggered in behind everyone else, laden with her cocker spaniel puppy's cage.

"He's a little hyper today," she announced, laying the cage against the wall.

"No problem," the teacher responded.

"Okay, let's take roll. Where are Katie and Lisa?"

"Katie's waiting for the baby, and Lisa's waiting for her dog," came the reply.

"Well, okay," the teacher stammered. "Now, let's get ready for the skits. If you have a costume, put it on now."

Kids sprang from their seats, and chaos ensued. Just then Katie sauntered into the classroom bouncing the baby on her hip.

"His name is Adam," she said as she handed him to the teacher. "And I need you to hold him while I put on my costume." He took the baby in his arms and tried to restore order. Ten minutes and many threats later, he regained control.

The first skit began. It was Gabrielle's group. "I feel so melancholy," she lamented, "because my dog is missing."

The kids performed the skit with unrivaled virtuosity. Meanwhile, the teacher rocked the baby in his lap as he observed and took notes. Just as the skit was approaching the climax when the puppy would dash from the cage into Gabrielle's loving arms, the classroom door burst open and in bounded a behemoth black lab, dragging Lisa behind it.

"Ahh!" squealed the students in unison. The puppy erupted from its cage and pounced upon the hellish lab. One fell swoop of the lab's paw sent the puppy flying across the room. Chaos ensued once more. Kids leapt from their desks, howling with glee. The group of performers barked their indignation at the dramatic interruption. Meanwhile, the battle for canine supremacy raged on, while Lisa and Gabrielle tried desperately to wrench the dogs apart. And the once-proud, now-fallen teacher rushed about the room trying to restore order while comforting the frightened infant in his arms.

Finally, the Bacchic revelry subsided. The battered puppy was thrust into its cage, and the victorious lab sat aloofly at Lisa's feet. The skits continued, but the teacher took no notice. He merely slouched at his desk rocking the baby and staring vacantly in front of him. The last skit ended, and the performers passed out Girl Scout Thin Mints to their classmates. The leftover cookies were placed in front of the black lab, who after a good long sniff, began to devour them. The teacher jerked alert, looked at the dog, and said with trepidation, "Wait, aren't dogs not supposed to eat chocolate?"

Just then the lunch bell rang, and the legion of demoniac seventh graders dashed for the door. Katie grabbed the baby and followed her classmates. Finally, Lisa headed out, pulling her dog behind. All of a sudden, the teacher noticed a small stream of brownish liquid coming from the tail end of the dog. Thin Mint induced diarrhea.

"Oh my God!" Lisa exclaimed as she turned around. "Sorry!" she yelled as she ran for the door, fearful of spending her lunch hour cleaning the stained carpet.

The despondent teacher observed the wreckage that was once his classroom. Props and costumes lay strewn about the floor; desks were overturned; the pungent scent of dog excrement wafted through the air. The teacher sighed, found a piece of paper, and scribbled some words on it. He then picked himself up and trudged mournfully out of the room. Before going to search for a sponge, bucket, and cleanser, he taped his newly-made sign to the door, echoing Dante's famous phrase: "Abandon hope all ye who enter here."

Refined Elegance

Kate Sullivan  ACE 8 Jackson

It didn't take long for me to realize my seventh-period Spanish I class of students, ranging from freshmen to seniors, would be a group that would challenge all my Harry Wong principles on a daily basis. This group of students, most of them born and raised in Jackson, Mississippi, had never really met someone from New York, let alone been taught by one such determined young lady who in reality was only four short years older than her most senior student. Perhaps being mistaken for a transfer student at orientation should have been a sign that commanding respect in the classroom would have to come in a form other than just looking the part of teacher. Armed with lesson plans and a title of "Señorita," the adventure began.

In the chaos of the first month, as I struggled to establish classroom management, keep my sanity, and reflect daily on ways I could improve, my first observation by the almost majestically wise Doc Doyle occurred. As I moved through my lesson, Doc observed the tightrope that was my subtle power struggle with a band of sophomore boys that not only could sense my vulnerability but also keenly strike when the timing was just right.

When chatting with Doc after class, it became apparent that the harshest critic in the room was not he, who possessed more knowledge of teaching high school-aged students than any educator coast to coast, but myself. As if it just happened, I still hold tightly to the simple but yet powerfully poignant compliment he paid me that day. He said, "Kate, you teach with a refined elegance that I have seen in no other young teacher." Nearly falling on deaf ears, for this was a girl who was still red in the face from just sweating through the last fifty minutes, he said it to me again. And from that day on, little by little, I started believing in the person that was leading the class. And on those most frustrating days where I felt more like I was leading a circus than a classroom, repeating Doc's compliment and channeling my inner Jackie Onassis, a calm, assured and proud dignity would take over and the learning would once again commence.

I don't still have a copy of the evaluation that Doc gave me that day, but I do have the post-it note on which I wrote the words, "refined elegance." Doc might have been just trying to make a teacher out of me on that day, but his words laid the foundation for the confident leader that I have become and continue to strive to be in all aspects of my life.

Gratitude

K.C. Kenney  ACE 12 Mobile

"Would you say a decade of the rosary?"

The pastor was at my side. He whispered in the crowded church, and looked around, hoping not to disturb other people praying. I looked up at Father from my knees, hands still folded from their mid-prayer. He had a young face, and at that moment it conveyed the weight he carried—weight of the responsibility he had as pastor and the grief that he was sharing with the Johnson Family.

"Of course," I whispered, quickly and with assurance. He thanked me and went on to the other preparations that were needed before the funeral began. I turned forward again, intending to continue my prayer, but was stifled by the myriad of thoughts that raced through my mind. What if I forgot the words? How could I possibly comfort my students? What would I do if I lost my own mother? How could something like this happen?

It was a Thursday morning in early December. I was usually teaching eighth-grade history at this time, but instead my class was sitting in the pews beside and behind me, quiet for once. We had come to pay our respects and to offer whatever comfort we could. The Sunday night before, the mother of Sarah, one of my seventh graders, had gone to bed complaining of coughing and chest pains. She got up in the middle of the night, apparently to use the restroom, but was found the next morning, having passed away from a heart attack. I remembered the shock I had felt hearing about it Monday morning, the disbelief, the confusion. All of that had to be set aside, now, because Sarah needed people to be there for her. When I first started teaching, this was exactly the kind of incident that I always wondered how I would face, but prayed that I would never have to find out.

I stood from the pew, took a glance at my class, straightened my black tie, and buttoned my black suit coat, and wandered to the back sacristy, in search of a rosary. As I reached the back of church, I saw Sarah coming in from the parking lot, surrounded by family and friends. I stood by the door, ready and willing to offer a kind word or a hug. I wracked my brain as she approached, but couldn't escape the knowledge that there weren't words that could offer comfort at such a time of grief.

The service continued without incident. I remembered all the words to the Hail Mary; was able to comfort my other students as they began to slowly break down, one by one, at the sight of one of their own experiencing such pain, such loss; and found myself tearing up as Sarah struggled to read a poem for her mother. I tried to think back to that age—a time when one feels so invincible yet so vulnerable at the same time.

As the service ended I joined the line of mourners, paying their respects to Mrs. Johnson, and showing their sympathy for Mr. Johnson and Sarah. I shook his hand and gave her a brief but sincere hug, told them both how sorry I was and that they would be in my prayers. I walked back to the classroom with the rest of my students and did my best to go about the day, trying to offer some semblance of normalcy in such a difficult situation.

But this was only the beginning of a very long day. A day filled with opposites, knowing that even as I said good-bye to Mrs. Johnson, that evening I would be greeting close friends that I hadn't seen since the summer. As the students filed out to catch their rides home, I tried to prepare to travel that night to Austin for the ACE December Retreat. I looked forward to the reunion that night as a chance to find some semblance of joy in an otherwise gloomy and mournful day.

The rest of ACE Mobile and I flew together from Mobile to Houston, where we waited for our connecting flight to Austin. In the airport, en route from one gate to the other, we bumped into other ACE teachers from all over the country, coming together to travel the last leg to Austin. Feeling pensive and a little down, I separated from the group with Char, a fellow ACE 12 from Pensacola, and began the walk to the next gate.

She asked me about my black suit and black tie, as I had not had an opportunity to change out of the funeral attire. Although the tie was loosened around the neck after such a stress-filled day, I still stood out among the other ACErs in jeans and December sweaters. Char joked a little about it, assuming I was dressing differently to be odd, and her face fell a little when I explained I hadn't had time to change after the funeral. As we boarded a train to carry us to the next terminal, I told her about my day.

Standing among long-distance commuters in business suits and a soldier still in fatigues, probably on his way home from some assignment, I opened up and it all came rushing out. The pain, the sadness, the despair. Not knowing how to speak to the father. Not knowing what to say to Sarah, or to the rest of my class. Not knowing how to teach in a classroom where no one was thinking about the subject matter.

The train arrived at our terminal, and we disembarked in relative silence, having said all I could think of to say. I felt a tap on my arm. I turned, and there stood the soldier.

"Excuse me, are you a teacher?"

Caught more than a little off guard, I responded without really thinking. "Why, yes, I am."

"I just want to thank you for what you do."

Time seemed to stop. The background faded away as I looked at this man, as though for the first time. Here was this guy, this soldier, dressed in fatigues and clearly either coming or going from some kind of duty.

And he was thanking me.

In some part of my mind, I decided he had overheard me talking to Char about my day and thought to speak up. Another part of my mind thanked God for the message. And still another part couldn't help but wonder, who the heck am I to be thanked for anything?

Time seemed to stand still. My mind reached out for something and grabbed hold of an image that moved me the first time I saw it and now took on even greater significance. There was a commercial a few years back, for Anheuser-Busch of all things. A group of soldiers are coming home from service abroad. They walk through a crowded airport, together, kind of standing out, still in fatigues themselves. And a slow clap begins. Soon, the entire airport terminal is applauding this small group of our nation's protectors. A traveler shakes one of the soldier's hands. And your heart swells. And you feel pride and gratitude for these great men and women that put their lives on the line. Whether you agree with the war or not, you must admit that they are brave. And they stand for something noble.

As I stood there in that airport in Houston, it was that image that flashed

The Spirit of ACE

through my mind. I was in shock. As much as I hope that each and every soldier receives the kind of reception portrayed in that short commercial, I had serious doubts that we lived in a world where something like that would be lived out in reality. And yet, it seemed that in that moment, in that airport, we did live in a world where the work of teachers was recognized. I struggled to wrap my mind around that contradiction. Here I was, enjoying the freedoms this man took part in protecting, but he had stopped me. He was recognizing me.

I was without words as I tried to reciprocate the sentiment. I felt awkward and lost. I felt so silly, trying to think about how to thank him in turn. But in my mind, it was like a lame comeback, "No, thank *you*."

So I simply said, "Thank you."

"Really, it's you guys who shape our future, and you do a lot."

"Thank you, I really appreciate it." Awkward. What could I say?

"With the state of education in our country, we need good people, doing good work."

"Yep, we're just trying to turn things around a bit." I was more or less blabbering at this point. I mean, what do you say?

"So, what Hell are you in?"

This I got. I recovered, laughed, and said, "Junior high." Evidently, he had a 14-year-old himself, who spent most of the time playing video games and fooling around.

He asked me my age. I told him, and he went on to comment how much younger than him that I was, and that kids respond well, need young role models, young teachers to see and with whom to interact. He reminisced briefly about a teacher from when he was in high school who only showed Hitchcock movies to teach elements of stories—conflict, theme, etc.

We came to a fork in the road and parted ways. And Char just said, "Wow. I'm glad I was there to witness that."

We talked about it for a few moments more, the gravity of the encounter. He'll probably never understand how much his words meant to me. He had no idea about the day that I had, where I was coming from, about the funeral, the students, the pressure, the grief, the struggle. For him it was probably just a moment. For me, it was a moment that I will never forget. With that, we walked on to meet the rest of our group.

What a way to start the weekend. ✪

Teaching

Eight Hundred Sets of Eyes

Katelyn Rosa  ACE 6 Brownsville

At least eight hundred sets of eyes were fixed on me. I stood at the podium in the middle of a high school auditorium. It was eerily silent and filled with people that were anxiously waiting for me to speak. What was I supposed to say? Just five months earlier, I was in college and never could have imagined being in this situation. Now, I was three months into my first year as an ACE teacher in rural, South Texas. It was going well, but this was definitely not what I had signed up for.

Rewind to a week earlier when one of the seniors from the Campus Ministry class approached me about reading at the school-wide prayer service. It was a monthly event where students, faculty, administrators, and parents were invited to gather and worship together; classes were even shortened to accommodate the event, so it was a big deal. I was honored that the students asked me—the "cool, new, young teacher"—to participate and figured that it would be easy enough to do a simple reading at the Thanksgiving service. I was trying to integrate myself into the spirit of the school and figured that it would be an ideal opportunity to be an active member of the community and do just that.

When the prayer service began, I noticed that there was no officiate at the Mass. I thought that was strange and briefly wondered who would be giving the homily. In the horribly awkward moment of silence after I finished my reading, it became clear to me who was supposed to give the homily: me. In a bit of a panic my eyes darted from the principal to the teacher in charge of Campus Ministry; it quickly became clear to them that I had not been sufficiently briefed about my role in the prayer service. They also realized that I had absolutely no idea what to do or say for the next forty-five minutes. The student that had accidentally forgotten to tell me that I was responsible for presenting the Thanksgiving homily to the entire school community shrugged and mouthed an apology that he was sorry he forgot to tell me. He figured that I somehow just knew that the teacher the students picked to do the reading usually did the homily as well. Welcome to the world of seventeen-year-olds!

As I looked around confused and befuddled, the situation became clear to the audience as well that I was not prepared to speak. They started nervously clapping, I think to show their support for me and to give me time to collect my thoughts. So I did just that. I took quite a few deep breaths, tried not to show how violently my hands and knees were shaking, and I started to speak. It was kind of a blur after that and I'm still not sure exactly what I said. However, many people approached me at the end of the service to applaud my effort. One teacher even used my experience as an example when she taught extemporaneous speaking later that week.

In retrospect I feel like many of my ACE experiences were extemporaneous on a regular basis! Nonetheless, I remember back to that day and those two years and I feel proud. I didn't always make it through with as much preparation as I would have liked, but I did make it through and I learned how to adapt and thrive. My ACE school community was an integral part of that.

As an ACE teacher it was easy at times to feel clueless and like an outsider; I certainly felt that way with eight hundred sets of eyes fixed on me. However, that feeling was often minimized by the affirmation that I received from my school community. I received it that day when they encouraged me through their applause and on so many days which are too numerous to count. That's the beauty of the ACE experience: it is multi-faceted and has more of an impact than you ever really realize.

Cross Country Czar

William Priestley  ACE 12 Biloxi

I remember one incident in particular that struck a chord with me during my time as an ACE teacher in Pascagoula, Mississippi. The event epitomized the resolve and perseverance that was synonymous with my school community in the wake of Hurricane Katrina. It took place at the first cross country meet of the season in Biloxi, where I was making my debut as coach.

How I ended up as the cross country coach was an interesting story in itself, as I tended not to like running unless there was something behind me. That aside, this particular day in September was typically scorching, and my middle school athletes began the competition already drained and exhausted. Fortunately, every member of our team acquitted themselves well among fervent competition, and with seemingly all our runners accounted for after the race, we began to assemble for a group picture.

We soon realized, however, that we were one man down. After a brief search we realized that Tim was still out on the course. Hurrying over to the slightly wooded area behind the stadium, we found Tim entering the final stretch of the course. He was flanked by his father who was urging him on, one step at a time. By this time, Tim had been sick and was clearly suffering from the heat. I immediately began to worry for his safety and whether he was going to make it another step, let alone another 2,000 to the end. We doused him in water and I had a quiet word with his father. I was genuinely concerned about the situation, but Bill simply said, "He'll make it," and that was the end of my doubt. There was something about his father's conviction and the manner in which Tim refused to give up, despite the slew of challenges ahead. It was an uncanny resolve in the face of adversity.

On we went, painfully at times, with sweat flowing in streams, skin glowing a fire engine red and muscles burning with lactic acid. Of course, these were just my own symptoms; I can only imagine what Tim was going through. Throughout this experience it was not only Tim's character but also that of the team that began to show. Everyone rallied around Tim and either walked, ran or jogged beside him on his journey. For a long time there seemed to be no end in sight, but for all my doubt, Tim never wanted to give up. I'm not sure how much body weight we had lost through perspiration by the time we came around that final corner, but it must have been several pounds. It was 110 degrees by my Irish thermometer and yet Tim pounded the dirt path beneath his feet as if he were beginning the race.

By this stage, most of the race markings had been taken down and the finish line all but disassembled. The awards ceremony had begun in the background and the majority of the team tents had been tidied away until the next week. As Tim entered the final straight, our team had lined what was left of the finish line to witness a truly remarkable achievement. As a fitting crescendo to his performance Tim sprinted the last 75 yards as if his life depended on it. It was just one of those moments when you're proud to be a coach, not in the sense that you are responsible for instilling such determination, but rather that you are present to witness it. On the back of our cross country t-shirts we had a quote printed paraphrasing the famous runner Steve Prefontaine. It read, "Some people run to see who is the fastest, I run to see who has guts." I felt that said it all. ✪

Precipitation

Marshall Davidson ACE 12 Los Angeles

These words were written the spring break of my second year in ACE and were preceded by an intense day wading through a cave in Guatemala. My hope in this poem was to express something about connection and possibility.

Grip gringo grime
Mist substance lime
In storm I drove
Constructed cave's cove
Ran through hemoglobin stream
Shined eye's gleam
Provide life essential coal
Choked breath of submarine soul
Prefer mother's purity
But mettle in men's absurdity
Slipped off Niagara's brow
Combined with leaf for Chairman Mao
Stagnated in Depression lows
Absent in Dust Bowl woes
On shores hosted Macbeth
Baptized King of Nazareth
Swatted Athenian Gadfly
Consumed PT-109
Transformed youth into blood filled puddles
When differences proved beyond subtle

The Spirit of ACE

Persian and Greek at Marathon
In abundance at Manhattan's prom
When destruction given break
Fertility in possibility's rake
When Mahatma ordered crown to halt
Joined Satyagraha in release of salt
Current of August '63 blitz
Flooded lungs of Auschwitz
Powered revolution of steam
Rest in nostalgic dream
Consecrated Assisi's glass
Desecrated Romero's Mass
In Pompeii, motioned civilization's abort
In Venice, allowed its transport
Fueled Luftwaffe's Guernica hush
Joined hues with Picasso's brush
In rivers, cleansed human failing
Left at center of heart's ailing
As
Liquid, solid, gas
In hydrological pass...
Just a drop
Not an actor
But a prop

The Virtue of Humility

Kelly (Perry) Buyske ● ACE 9 Tucson

I'm not great with names, and I've been known to get my words twisted now and again. Is it "biting at the chomp" or "chomping at the bit?" I am definitely one of those people who will for years sing the wrong lyrics to a song, and was quite sure that Janis Joplin was singing "Windshield wipers, turpentine. I was holding Bobby's hand in mine," never noticing that Janis really didn't need the turpentine, nor did it belong in her song. My sons, William and Benedict, are surely going to get tired of their mother mixing their names up, but I'm not willing to just call out, "Hey you!" Yet, all of these shortcomings, or "cute idiosyncrasies that make me loveable," as I prefer to call them, certainly played out hilariously in the classroom during my years as a fourth-grade teacher at Santa Cruz School in Tucson.

I can vividly recall one slip of the tongue. It was early in the school year and I was discussing homework habits with my nine- and ten-year-old students. As I patrolled the classroom, looking at the homework efforts, and realizing I had just created hours of work for myself, I tried to impress upon these youngsters the importance of taking the time to complete their homework carefully.

I asked a series of questions: Each night, did they make sure that they had enough space to spread out all of their materials? Would they use the homework planner that we filled out each afternoon? Before they sat down to get to work, did they make sure that there were no distractions in the room that would break their concentration? I asked them to tell me what things could make them lose their focus while trying to read or figure out math problems. Television. Good. Loud music. Yes. Annoying little sisters. Okay.

They seemed to get the picture, so I decided to recap. "So, when you sit down to do your homework, make sure you can focus. Just get anything that might distract you out of your way. Clear off your work space, turn off the TV and computer games, and put down the *Playboy* and get to work!"

Hold on a second, I thought to myself. That didn't sound quite right, did it? Then I realized my mistake. Of course, I'd meant to say Game Boy. It was one of those times where I prayed none of the kids knew what I'd just said, and I was about to rush on when my favorite little troublemaker, Tony, piped right up.

"Yeah, that would be distracting, Miss Perry!"

Thanks for that, Tony. Coming to my rescue, making sure I am humbled, yet again, by kids who have yet to figure out how to do long division and can't write in cursive.

The Greatest Teacher

Tom Jacobs ★ ACE 2 Oklahoma City

Theo was a junior and senior during my two years as an ACE teacher. While he was a student in my basic chemistry class from the very beginning, I have vague early recollections of him. Theo was an average kid, not outstanding in any activity or subject, excelling only at being average. Theo defined average. He neither actively participated during class discussions nor was he intrusively distracting. He would be in his seat when the bell rang, occupy his space for the fifty minutes, and then quietly move on through his schedule. The only friend I noticed with him was, in many respects, the polar opposite of Theo. Blair was as noticeable as Theo was invisible. She was loud, obnoxious, and distracting. Theo often appeared amused by Blair's antics and would give her subtle encouragement, but even with Blair, Theo never lost his individuality. Rather than being Blair's shadow, Theo was often eclipsed by Blair's brighter personality, as if his intention were to be with someone who took the attention away from him. While it seemed that Theo was generally regarded well by his peers and could have been one of the in-crowd, it seemed that he intentionally chose against popularity. Even with Blair, Theo remained a self-defined individual and a loner.

His participation in my class was below expectation. While he would not be a disruption in class, he rarely actively participated or completed homework and did not make studying for tests a regular part of his schedule. My first real interaction with Theo came shortly after mid-way through the first quarter, just after progress reports were issued. Theo came to me during my lunch break in near tears. His parents had informed him that if he did not make significant improvements in my class, he would be grounded. I told Theo that I empathized with his situation, and that I would assist him with any assignment with which he struggled, but it was not my habit to "give" grades; whatever grade he received was the grade he earned. I did, however, encourage him, expressed my faith in him, and offered any future help whenever he felt he needed it. Hopefully, I left the impression that we were in this together and that I desired him to be successful. I hope that was the impression I left.

Theo caught my attention again late in that first semester, earning my respect and admiration one afternoon at an all-school assembly. I do not remember the purpose of the assembly, but I vividly remember his address at its conclusion. At the request of the campus minister, Theo made an appeal to the student body to take advantage of the spiritual aspect of the high school. Though the request had been made of him, he was provided no text or format; what he said were his own words, and it caught me as the most authentic and profound appeal I had ever heard. Roughly, he stated, "We're fortunate enough to attend a school with access to a chapel. Anyone who chooses to not spend at least a couple of minutes between classes in that chapel every day is a fool."

His statement was unapologetic and definitive. No one dared challenge it. Theo stated it as a fact of which he himself was convicted, and all of his audience—his peers and his mentors—seemed to accept his statement on the authority of his confidence. I even remember feeling a pang of guilt for having not visited the chapel recently. I had never previously witnessed such confidence expressed in one's faith, such genuine, authentic confidence, as this young man had just displayed. Honestly, it seemed to me to be the ultimate un-cool thing to do. No one would have been able to convince me at his age to stand in front of an auditorium filled with my peers and urge the activity of prayer. It would have been social suicide! But this kid was beyond reproach. He was not looking for approval or support. He was simply stating the truth as he knew it, and he stated it so well that I half expected the auditorium to empty as the student body stampeded to the chapel.

During the remainder of his high school career, I had the opportunity to interact with Theo in various activities, including campus ministry events. However, it was not until after he graduated that I learned the story behind the kid. Theo had just graduated and I, too, was moving on. Over a farewell cup of coffee, Theo shared his story with me.

His dad was a stereotypic jock and desperately desired his son to follow in his footsteps. When Theo quit the football team during his freshman year of high school, his dad was furious. He insisted that as his son, he would, indeed, play football. Theo, at age fourteen, replied, "Dad, I'm gay. I don't feel right watching the other guys undress in the locker room." His dad had little to do with him after that. His mother's response was, "You can call me by my first name, but don't call me Mom."

After hearing Theo's story, I began to understand how this "kid" could stand in front of a crowd of his peers and risk rejection by unabashedly stating his faith and convictions. In many instances in the ten years since I had that conversation with Theo, I have found courage and inspiration through his example. Through his unwavering dedication to authenticity, integrity, faith, and courage, that child, that young man would prove to be, and continues to remain, one of my greatest teachers. I am sure I gained more from his example than he ever learned from my instruction, and I really do not care if he learned any chemistry. ✪

Never Give Up

Dominic Yonto ACE 12 St. Petersburg

I coached many different teams in my two years in ACE, but my favorite coaching experience was the middle school JV basketball team. I remember going into our first game against Christ the King thinking we had a pretty good team. I also remember driving home after getting beat 52-0 thinking I couldn't believe that anyone would show up to practice the next day.

Not only did my guys show up for practice, they showed up for our second game with an attitude. I was shocked as we were walking into the gym and hearing my bench players talking about how bad we were going to beat our opponent. My only response was, "Guys, let's just hit the backboard in this game." While we did score, we still lost by more than 30 points.

Our second to last game came down to the last minute of the fourth quarter. I had not called a timeout the entire season because I figured it would help the other team more than it would help us. But I needed to draw up a play because we had a chance for the first time all season. It wasn't until I called the timeout that I realized I didn't even have a board to draw a play on. I had to walk over to the other team's huddle and ask their coach to borrow his. While the play worked to perfection, the shot landed in the fourth row of the bleachers.

Again, I expected my players to be crushed, but they were more excited than ever. We had a great week of practice and returned to the same gym to face Concordia Lutheran for a second time. Things were a little different this time. Our starting point guard was sick, which meant my backup, Nate, who was not normally allowed to touch the ball, would run what we called an offense.

The game was close. Concordia never led by more than three points. We never led. Until, with one minute to go, we in-bounded the ball under our own hoop to Nate. As soon as he got the ball I knew what he was going to do. He crossed half court with a twinkle in his eye, and me screaming at him not to shoot. This four-foot-tall sixth grader launched the ball from hip level, two steps on our side of half-court, as I was yelling "Nooooooooooo" at the top of my lungs. Then, of course, the ball went in.

With my team running in circles, I tried to get them back to play defense for the last minute of the game. Somehow Concordia never scored, despite our team never returning to their positions. The time ran out and my team continued to run in circles, while I was yelling at them to, "Line up! Act like you've won before!" As I attempted to gather my winning team, one of my players, Michael, ran by and said, "But coach, we don't know what to do. We have never won before." I couldn't help myself, standing there laughing I told Michael, "Line up, shake hands, then we'll go nuts."

Winning the last game of the season was great. It really lifted the confidence of my sixteen middle schoolers. This group of fifth and sixth graders embodied resiliency. Despite a terrible loss to start the season they did not give up. As they continued to lose, they continued to hustle and work hard in practice. When good players got into trouble, others picked up slack. Despite losing to a team in the second to last game, they never gave up. With odds stacked against them, this team willed its way to a win. Seeing the smiles, watching them run in circles, being congratulated by the parents you would have thought we had a winning season. The lessons learned were not about a 2-3 zone or a good form shot. The lesson that my team and I learned together was to never give up. ✪

The Motivation Debate

Michael Macaluso ACE 11 Baton Rouge

Though it has been nearly four years since my first summer in ACE, I still remember the day in our High School Methods class that Doc hit us with his belief that teachers cannot motivate students. It will forever be emblazoned in my head because it was the day all of our idealistic bubbles broke and we woke to a reality that was not yet real for us. Doc loved it, of course, as he smiled with his typical pose of hand under chin.

He calmly called on each one of us, willing to let the debate ensue, as we fired our counterarguments at him. No one agreed with him, yet he handled it with unparalleled cool, confidence, and charisma. We weren't angry with Doc, nor did we hold it against him that he could be such an outstanding educator and still believe such nonsense. Instead, we embraced Doc, as everybody does, and "beat on, boats against the current" into the gauntlet of the high school classroom, ready to prove him wrong.

After four years of teaching high school students, I am still not willing to concede to Doc, although I do admit that he was partially right. Teachers can only create the atmosphere for learning, encourage the students, and let them take control of their own education. At the same time, there has to be potential for one person to motivate another, especially in an atmosphere of respect, rapport, and learning. I witnessed this during my time in ACE in Baton Rouge, Louisiana, and now I see something similar at my high school alma mater in the suburbs of Chicago. My ACE school and my current school are incredibly different, yet my experiences at both still provide evidence for my theory.

At the Senior class retreat during my second year of teaching in Baton Rouge, one of my students, Kurt, told the group that he was planning on majoring in

Business and American Literature because of "Mr. Mac's English class." Hearing Kurt say this was an incredible moment for me because I had battled with him all year, knowing he had the capability to blow his peers out of the water if he only had the motivation.

As he stood there, proudly announcing what he wanted to study in college, I remembered the day I called his mother to talk to her about his potential. She began sobbing with me on the phone because she was going through a difficult time and Kurt was her only support. Hearing Kurt speak about my class in that way on retreat meant more to me than any stellar in-class work my students may have completed. It meant more than his getting a 98% on the next test he took after I spoke with his mom; it meant more to me than his understanding the symbolism in a Hawthorne short story; and it meant more to me than his producing a nearly perfect research paper. On some level, I reached one of my students despite our difficulties, and I am grateful for having had him in class.

With respect to Doc's theory of motivation, I recognize and fully admit that there are those students who will do nothing in our classes. Not every situation is like my encounter with Kurt. Some students are more than happy to tell me that they hate my class or don't understand the bigger picture of what I am trying to teach them. Some have continually not completed or turned in assignments, no matter the detriment to their grade, their summer plans, their future. Why is it that some students can so aptly respond to an appropriate work environment and some choose to surrender to mediocrity before the battle has even begun?

Beyond the debate about motivation, I often wonder how I can better connect with my students, and through that relationship, encourage them to learn to the best of their ability. I reflect on the connection I had with my kids in Baton Rouge because I was the outsider who came in and helped them see their potential. Conversely, there are times when I am overcome with joy because the students I have now in Chicago will delve deep into a discussion and connect with me on literary themes and topics. Wherever I'm teaching, my hope is that my students respond to the positive atmosphere of my classroom and strive to work toward the high expectations I have set for them. Do I attribute their success to our connection? Is it motivation? Or is it a positive learning environment? Regardless of what it is, I am committed to uncovering that which helps my students reach their full potential.

My thoughts return to that first ACE summer, and how I'll never forget Doc's grin that day in High School Methods. I'm sure that deep down he ironically understands that we are motivated by his expectations and standards. With this in mind, I am not willing to give up on some of my students, nor am I willing to let my teaching, planning, and assessing take a back seat. If ACE has taught me anything, it is that anything is possible. The key to understanding motivation is there; I just don't have the experience to grasp it yet. But when I do, Doc will be the first to know.

To the Death

Mariaelena (Raymond) Amato ACE 7 Los Angeles

The first classes I ever taught were high school English classes in Montebello, California. I had three sections of freshmen and two of juniors. With approximately thirty students in each class, and a need to emphasize writing skills, I amassed a vast quantity of grading. One hundred forty-two papers, to be exact, and that's only if a one-page paper was required. With the other pressures of being a first-year teacher, grading was one more hurdle, but it was a very high hurdle. After creating lesson plans that very rarely extended beyond what I planned to do the following day, I would dive into my piles of papers and peck away at them into the early hours of the next morning.

My roommates were astounded by these papers. They took up a very visible presence in our apartment. Stacks were in the family room, the kitchen, my bedroom, my book bag. I never slept enough, and I never seemed to be able to grade enough.

My angel of good advice came in the form of a former nun who told me the following story about a sister in her order. We'll call her Sister Grace. Here is her story.

Like me, Sister Grace had a lot of grading to do. One evening, her fellow sisters asked her to join them for an evening out. Sister Grace indicated the piles of papers at her feet with a wave of her hand, sadly shook her head, and said, "I'm sorry, but I really need to grade these." Her sisters left without her, and they enjoyed a wonderful dinner.

Upon their return, they found Sister Grace's papers neatly stacked, every single paper corrected, everything in order. Sister Grace lay beside them all—dead.

The Spirit of ACE

    The former nun spelled out the moral of the story for me. She said very plainly, "Mariaelena, don't grade everything. If you grade everything, you'll die." I have taken this very sound advice to heart. I have stayed in teaching. While I no longer teach English, and while I have much smaller classes, I have learned how to leave my piles of grading behind.

    I look forward to a much longer life. ✪

Miracle on San Felipe Street

Laura Aull  ACE 10 San Antonio

As it was December, it was still dark out though school would begin in less than an hour. Straightening the handouts to be passed out for the day, I stopped for a moment to consider the specific handout in my hand: the fall exam review sheet. The end of the semester.

It had been a long first few months: transitions, challenges, students who did not have the academic resources and support I had once taken as a given part of education, students with so many hopes and so far to go. And on this particular December morning I recalled one fall afternoon that semester when I had sat down, stared upward, and realized what it was I had felt in the pit of my stomach for weeks: I was genuinely unsure if I could actually do what I was supposed to do for these students.

I had never taught before. I was in an all-male high school serving the Mexican-American Westside of San Antonio. I was very young, and neither Mexican nor male. I wasn't sure how well I or they could know what each other's lives and prior knowledge were, or exactly what knowledge we were seeking now. I knew I was distant and strict because I felt I didn't have an alternative, but I also knew that students needed to trust me, needed to know that their teacher cared about more than their writing and reading skills. Was I reaching them? Was I serving their truest needs?

My thoughts were interrupted by a knock at the door. José, a senior student of mine, was at the doorway, wearing a broad, proud grin as his brown-green eyes widened with energy. I motioned that he could open the door, surprised by such an early arrival.

"Good morning, José!"

"Good morning, Miss. Are you going to be in here for the next few minutes?"

Once I had assured him I would be, I continued with my preparations as he disappeared through the doorway again. A few minutes later, José and several other students were at my door again, this time carrying something I had mentioned in passing that I would not have for Christmas that year: a real, live Christmas tree. Bursting with the smell of pine and my faraway home and complete with a classic red and green metal base, the tree was guided in and set to stand seven feet tall in the corner of my classroom. Lights and ornaments were furnished by other junior and senior students, wearing smiles hanging somewhere between bashful awkwardness and deliberate charm.

One of the students hanging ornaments joked with me that they were "Shakespeare ornaments." He was the same student who, two weeks before, had received a curt talking to from me for putting his head down several times in a class period. I found out soon afterward that just before my class, he heard that his family's house was broken into again that morning by a drug addict; the house had again been robbed and damaged. After school I told him I was so sorry that had happened, not knowing what else to do.

As I watched them, humbled and utterly surprised, I wondered if they would ever know how grateful I was. I wondered if they would ever know that because of them, I learned what real service is—that sincere reaching out amidst the puzzled human ways we try to know others, all cradled somehow in grace.

Soon the setup was complete and the tree plugged in. For the remaining days of the semester, all one could see through the windows, blazing through the bars into the tepid December air, were the blend of white lights and ornaments, and the shadow of the needles of the tree branches, climbing like fingers up the wall and warmly illuminating the Westside bricks outside.

I keep one of those ornaments in my desk now, years later, as I pursue my Ph.D. in work I hope will make a difference in the lives of students like those guys. I pick it up periodically, and it seems to say what I learned and re-learned every day of my years in ACE: It is precious, backward poetry that when we serve, we are the ones who gain, and that those who have almost nothing to give, so often give the most.

Answered Prayer

Francisco Ramirez — ACE 11 Kansas City

I had the privilege of serving at All Saints Catholic School in Kansas City, Kansas. I spent three years teaching there and I took with me stories that will forever be in my heart. I also took stories that I don't like to remember because they prove to be too painful. We know that every school has at least one student who every teacher knows by name. These are the students who challenge us and make our life miserable. "Without him or her," we always say, "my class would be perfect!" These students are also the ones that make being a teacher worth it.

Jason was one of those students. He was a new student assigned to my class in January, but he was so behind academically and socially that we moved him to third grade a couple of weeks into the year. He was notorious and constantly in trouble. I, of course, was not looking forward to having him in my classroom the following fall. Maybe they would assign him to the other fourth-grade class, I thought. God would not have it that way.

We started the year on good terms. However, he was a constant behavior problem, and I was getting frustrated because I could not mold him as I was able to do with my other students. He did not fit my mold. I was constantly on him and made sure he did not get away with anything. It felt like babysitting rather than teaching.

I will forever remember the day I lost it. It had been a long day and he was acting up again. He came to my desk, and I told him to sit back down. He, of course, did not do as I asked and started touching things on my desk. Jason accidentally hit my family picture frame, and it went crashing down. I remained quiet as I saw my frame broken on the floor. He then looked at me and told me he did not do it. That was it. I could not believe my ears. I started yelling at him and belittling him out of frustration. The class remained silent. I caught myself, stopped, and looked the other way and started to pray. I felt horrible. I told him to sit back down; I picked up my frame and calmed down.

The rest of the day I felt uneasy. How could I have lost it that bad, I asked myself. I had the power to encourage and strengthen, and I had chosen neither. I went to Mass after school and prayed for guidance, patience, and understanding. I wanted to love Jason and treat him like I did my other students, regardless of his behavior or attitude.

I went to daily Mass and continued praying for him and for myself. About a week later, school did not serve lunch so students had to bring their own lunch from home. I, like many other times, forgot mine. As students ate their lunches in the classroom, I walked around and told them I had eaten a big breakfast and was not hungry. I got to Jason's table, and he pulled out two sandwiches. He grabbed one and gave it to me. "My mom made one for you and one for me, Mr. Ramirez," he told me. I could not look at him; I was taken aback and shocked. This was no coincidence. My prayers had been answered in this small way. Jason was special and I needed to get past my preconceived notions in order to realize this. I needed him and God to open my eyes and help me see the wonder that was this student.

I took the sandwich, thanked him, turned around and prayed a Hail Mary in thanksgiving. The rest of the year was a lot better. We got along and worked well together. I still see him and he always makes it a point to come over and shake my hand. Little does he know that his handshake means the world to me.

Teaching: The Art of Persuasion

Fr. Ronald Nuzzi ✪ ACE Leadership Director

As a part of the required formation program for all priesthood candidates, my seminary required what was known as an "apostolic work." Scheduled during weekends or on evenings after class, apostolic work took the seminarian out of the confines of the seminary, and into the local church for some firsthand, but supervised ministry.

During the first six years of seminary, I had taught school, worked in youth ministry, confirmation preparation, parent classes for baptism, and various retreat efforts. I enjoyed them all and learned something in each experience, but by year seven, I was ready to do something different and new and challenging. I pored over the remaining options in the apostolic works catalogue—parish fundraising, divorce and annulment ministry, preparing liturgical ministers—without sensing any attraction at all, worried that this year would amount to nothing more than repeating a previous experience. But then, I spied one entry that caught my fancy: police chaplain. This apostolic work had the standard description, but it was followed by an asterisk. The accompanying footnote indicated that the head police chaplain had to interview all candidates for this position and that it was not simply a matter of signing up, as one did for all other apostolic works. One had to apply and be accepted for this position.

My interview went well. The head chaplain explained the ministry as consisting of accompanying a police officer in a patrol car, and assisting in situations such as accident and death notifications, domestic disputes, and civil disturbances, and generally being a support for the officer. The chaplain further added that the police department had come to rely on the chaplain corps in many of these situations, having had firsthand experience of the effectiveness of a chaplain's presence, in addition to a police officer, when delivering the news of a serious accident or death. There were four required training sessions, and if I completed them successfully, the chaplain said, the job was mine.

The training proved helpful, but uneventful, and I was on the job within two weeks. My first several shifts amounted to little more than getting to meet several potential partners, learning my way around the district headquarters, and securing some equipment and a locker.

The first, real chaplain activities I recall were accident notifications, mostly contacts with parents and extended families regarding an automobile accident of their teenage son, daughter, or grandchild. As these were all accident notifications and not death notifications, every parent without exception was relieved and grateful—relieved the report was of an accident and grateful that we came personally to tell them the details.

A few domestic disputes got my adrenaline flowing, but in each of those situations the officer in charge exercised so much authority as to make my presence unnecessary. There were more senseless and meaningless calls than I care to remember: lost keys, misplaced credit cards, sick pets, even UFO sightings. The experience created in me a more compassionate posture towards law enforcement, and helped me to see close up what I had heard others say before, albeit from a distance, namely, that the job was so dangerous precisely because it was so often innocuous immediately and for extended periods right before the true danger arrived. The excitement and energy of the work were directly connected to the complete and absolute mystery of what was coming next.

On one, cold February weekend—Valentine's Day weekend to be precise—I earned my stripes. We were called to a local White Castle, an inexpensive, late-night burger joint, to help settle an angry, dissatisfied customer who allegedly had threatened to drive his pick-up truck through the front entrance. Upon arrival, we learned that the young man had recently been jilted by his girlfriend, and the cashier in the White Castle who got his order wrong simply constituted the last straw. He was angry and was determined to take out his anger on the building. He had screamed his intentions to all who would listen and they had promptly vacated the building—patrons and employees alike. We found about a dozen people huddled in the parking lot when we arrived.

My partner did not even get out of the car. He pulled us up next to the truck so I could speak directly to the man behind the wheel without getting out of the police cruiser. His exact words to me were, "Chaplain, this one's all yours." When preliminary car-to-truck discussions went nowhere, I appealed to my partner to get out of the cruiser, but it was cold, bitter cold. He did, but treated it much like a traffic stop, approaching the truck from the rear, staying well behind the driver's door, and unbuckling but not drawing his firearm. The truck driver was angry and a bit irrational, but he was not armed. We did fear that he would follow through on his threat to drive into the building, so we did not attempt to remove him forcefully from the truck. A fruitless, somewhat disjointed conversation ensued for what seemed like a frustrating eternity. We had to go back into the police cruiser to warm up a bit and reconsider our strategy.

I asked my partner if he might shoot out the tires and disable the vehicle. He answered that the truck had enough power and was close enough to the building to drive it a few hundred feet even with flat tires. Moreover, he was not authorized to discharge his firearm for such a strategy. We thought about what might happen were the man to drive into the building and decided that a fire and an explosion were likely, given the gas grills and cooking apparatus close to the front counter. A truck accelerating through the parking lot could easily land in the middle of the cooking area, and coupled with the gasoline in the truck's tank, create an explosion and a fire. We called for the fire department to come to the scene and made a dramatic show of moving the patrons and employees to a safe distance. With the fire engines roaring in, sirens blazing, I had to play our bluff. "OK, pal, we're ready. You wanna drive into the building, do it. These people are at a safe distance now and the fire engines are here to put out the fire and to protect everyone from the explosion." The lead firefighter, perhaps being familiar with the ploy, offered his help. He threw a firefighter's jacket and head gear into the cabin of the truck, telling the driver to put them on for his own safety. He shouted directions about adjusting them properly so as to have the maximum protection from the fire and explosion.

The truck driver seemed to be getting it, understanding that everyone there was preparing for a serious explosion and fire. Other firefighters walked over to the crowd of employees and patrons, covering them with fire resistant blankets, and tossing over some protective head gear for good measure.

When the truck driver got out of the cabin in order to adjust his jacket and head gear, they also threw him some boots, and when he reached down to grab them, my partner tackled him and brought him down without incident or injury.

Arrested, handcuffed, and seated in the back seat of the police cruiser, the truck driver chided me as my partner completed some paperwork and radio calls. "What sort of chaplain school did you go to? Tellin' me to drive into the building. You're no chaplain. You're a fool!" I tried not to respond, but he asked me what chaplain school I went to at least a dozen times in two minutes. I finally gave in and told him I was studying to be a priest. He just shook his head.

The police chaplain gig never really got any better than that, but it was a night I will never forget. I do not think anyone could have talked this particular individual away from the truck with appeals to reason or logic. He had to be otherwise persuaded, met on his own terms, and invited to see the situation differently. It was a bluff, a calculated guess, and a bit of a white lie. He needed to change so that he could want what we wanted for him—to get out of there without hurting himself or others. We overstated our case, exaggerated a bit, and added in some dramatic moments for effect. Overall and in retrospect, it was some of the best teaching I have ever done and it happened at a White Castle on a cold Friday in February. ✪

Roots of Identity

Maria Loebig-Haberle  ACE 6 Nashville

It took more than twenty years for me to embrace my African roots. Literally. Like most Black women, I struggled with the kinky, nappy afro. I straightened and processed. I installed weighty, fake braids. I cried and agonized to achieve that White-woman-length hair that "moved" but eventually broke off. Tired of trying to pass for the more acceptable Latina—tired of trying not to look like a "slave" and be fully accepted into the White community—I shaved my hair into a short afro. There it was for the world to see. In case they should forget, there I was—Loebig, Black and free!

Notre Dame didn't forget: the ACE program placed me in Nashville in an all Black school. I figured it was a great chance to be the Black "role model," one who didn't become impregnated at the age of 15. The Black woman for whom education, travel, and following God's will was cool—the usual jazz. Ironically, my ACE school location ended up being mostly just a chance to represent symbolic locks. The longer I grew the fro, the more sensation it stirred within this Black community. It was a bizarre cultural experience. Some applauded me. Others referred me to their stylist. Every now and then, when I grew weary of the daily grooming with the fluorescent '80s style pick, I grabbed my Waul's electric shaver, sat on the balcony, and shaved it all again.

Towards the end of my tour of duty, I read *Nappy Hair* by Carolivia Herron to my eighth-grade language arts class. A great story for defining theme, main idea, tone, or creating short analyses, the entire work shines in its celebration of racial heritage. The book reads in the 1800s slave-like call and response format. Loveable patriarch, Uncle Mordecai, convinces the rest of his African-American family not to make fun of young Brenda's afro. Her hair, a gift from God, has endured the journey from Africa through hundreds of years of slavery to the contemporary day. Mordecai declares that it is not acceptable to straighten a perfect circle, much less make fun of it. He reminds the family that the afro was God's creation. And He rules the world—no matter how many angels and people complain.

Today as I sport my new style in dread locks, I have continued to read this children's book to all of my classes in three different states: Tennessee, Texas, and Pennsylvania. To some students, I could possibly symbolize the African-American woman who did not give into the "ghetto" lifestyle. However, the real influence occurs when Black female students and I engage in serious conversation about how hair can keep a woman from embracing her true self. Identity through one's hair, embracing one's crowning glory, accepting one's given self—this gift is one that many are not ready to accept. Others are tempted. Either way, it's a great way to explore the soul. Female and male students discuss who they want to be, either as people of color or people who must accept and celebrate other differences. Most importantly, students realize that they have the power to influence how others view them.

The Annex

Antonio Ortiz  ACE 5 Mission

Most college graduates have incredible opportunities lined up when they leave school and enter the proverbial real world. While I majored in business, and had several of these opportunities, I decided to participate in the Alliance for Catholic Education. For two years, I would live in the Diocese of Brownsville, Texas, and teach at a Catholic school.

Through the ACE Program, I found myself teaching fifth-, sixth-, seventh- and eighth-grade social studies, religion, algebra, pre-algebra, and journalism in a small K-8 grade school. With endless optimism, I showed up at St. Joseph Catholic School in early August, eager and ready, so I thought, to start the academic year. I had a Notre Dame degree in my hand; what could possibly go wrong?

My good friend and ACE roommate, Tim Green, often quoted Mark Twain in describing education as, "the path from cocky ignorance to miserable uncertainty." The stage of "cocky ignorance" didn't last long, however, and my "miserable uncertainty" began with the first unexpected challenge.

I was told that the school had run out of classroom space and that a solution was in the works. The solution, it turns out, was to rent a two-bedroom house two blocks away from the school and call it the "Education Annex." I was assigned the master bedroom, and with a few tables and chairs arranged in a rectangle, I was handed the keys to my first classroom. Another teacher who had seniority was assigned the coveted living room, which was the more spacious classroom in the Annex. Imagine, spending the entire day with middle school kids in a small, confined room, not even half the size of a typical classroom.

By October, the initial dismay of seeing my first classroom wore off, just in time to hear the news that I would now be switching content areas. As the frustration mounted with the faculty, the middle school math teacher decided to quit, so the principal asked me if I would consider picking up algebra and pre-algebra for the seventh and eighth grades. I told the principal I was not sure that I was really qualified to teach math and that, quite honestly, I remember struggling through algebra in high school. His reply was, "Great, it will just make you a better teacher because you'll be able to empathize with those students who struggle in math." Hardly the vote of confidence or answer I was looking for.

So, in the middle of my first semester, after teaching in a house for several months, I threw out my social studies curriculum and began writing math lessons. Finally, the day before Christmas break, the principal pulled me aside and told me "I just want to thank you for all you've done and it's been a pleasure working with you." I thought to myself, "Oh no, I'm getting canned." Well, it turns out I wasn't getting fired, the principal was actually quitting! He decided to jump ship before the ship sank, because indeed this school was sinking fast. My first semester was marked by teaching in a house instead of a classroom, changing content areas with little to no preparation, and witnessing several faculty and administrators quit. Only a year and a half left in this program. I began to wonder if any of those business consulting jobs were still available.

Needless to say, it did get better over the remaining year and a half I spent at St. Joseph Catholic School. And that is one of the many lessons I learned from my ACE experience: Never give up too early on what may seem like a bad situation. The school did eventually turn around under new leadership and, nine years later, is now thriving.

After a second ACE summer at Notre Dame, I returned to St. Joseph Catholic School, and was welcomed by Sr. Kathleen Murray, D.C., the school's third principal in as many semesters. The bravado I walked into St. Joseph Catholic School with the previous year was gone, replaced with many hesitations, questions, and fears. Sr. Kathleen, however, put many of those fears to rest when she walked me to my new classroom! Although it was a portable classroom, it was a step up from the house. The rest of that year would be filled with many of those moments of relief as Sr. Kathleen began the process of firmly rooting herself in the school community and bringing about real, sustainable leadership and positive change for the school. I recently spoke with Sr. Kathleen and she informed me the school has never been healthier. Since her arrival at St. Joseph's, enrollment has increased by almost fifty percent. The school recently completed a capital campaign that led to the construction of three new classrooms, and overall, the school atmosphere is rejuvenated and upbeat.

Sr. Kathleen attributes much of the revival at St. Joseph's to the ACE program which has committed teachers to the school for the last ten years. The ACE program would have had good reasons to leave the struggling school a decade ago, but on the contrary, it decided to send some of the program's most talented and committed teachers to assist in the turnaround. The enthusiasm, optimism, and energy that ACE teachers have brought to the school allowed Sr. Kathleen to build a respected mission-driven faculty that would demonstrate to the community that St. Joseph Catholic School is a magnificent institution that provides an opportunity for children to receive a quality education and at the same time develop their Catholic faith.

A Lesson in Church Hierarchy

Johnnie Quigley ✺ ACE 14 Dallas

The Diocese of Dallas named a new bishop, Kevin Farrell, and one of the first tasks he wanted to take on was to visit all the Catholic schools in the diocese. Our Lady of Perpetual Help, the school I was working in, just so happened to be one of the first on his list. I wasn't expecting the principal to take the bishop into my classroom because it was the second week of school and I was a first-year teacher, but in they walked—my principal, the superintendent of Dallas Catholic schools, and Bishop Farrell. I promptly blushed as red as I ever have before. As I was standing there, cheeks burning, I was glad that my students were able to get over their shock more quickly. Before the Bishop could walk to the front of the room or even introduce himself, my students started firing any questions that came to mind. I shrugged and laughed hoping they couldn't tell how uncomfortable I was. The Bishop seemed satisfied by my students' curiosity and left with my students still trying to spit questions at him as he walked out the door.

I survived that possible catastrophe with only blushing once and took my students into the computer lab. We were in the computer lab, and my students were desperately trying to learn how to type in URLs when the Bishop walks in again! I suppose my principal wanted to show off the computer lab Southwest Airlines had donated to our school only two years before, but did they really have to come and see it while my class was there? Instinctively, I blushed, but I was too flustered trying to help my students type in Web addresses to even worry about how red my face was. The bishop walked around and I saw him talking to students. He left and I was so relieved.

After he left, one of my students, Edward, turned to me and exclaimed, "Mrs.! Mrs.! Guess what?"

"What Edward?"

"The Pope helped me with my computer!"

I laughed a little and said, "That was actually the bishop not the pope, and I am 'Miss' not 'Mrs.,' but we'll talk about that later." ✪

Year of the Ducks

Amy Vanden Boogart ● ACE 11 Kansas City

My first year of teaching was the Year of the Ducks. It didn't start out as the Year of the Ducks though; it started out as the Hardest Year of My Life and it quickly became even harder than that. But then, slowly but surely, by the time school ended in May, it had become the Year of the Ducks.

You may be wondering what made my first year as a fifth-grade teacher the Year of the Ducks. It happened accidentally, really. I started out the school year by coming up with a different pet name for my students every day. I would call them my little kittens, my little cutie pies, my little explorers, my little this, my little that. One day, I just happened to call them my little duckies. I believe I said, "Good morning, my little duckies." Then, from somewhere in the back of the classroom, one of the duckies responded, "Good morning, Mother Ducky!" Well, that was it! From that moment on, I was the Mother Ducky, and my students were my Little Duckies, and this school year became the Year of the Ducks.

There's something about the symbolism of a mother duck and her duckies that just seems to fit a teacher and her students. The mother duck leads the way, finds the path across the pond, and tries to lead her children to safety. The duckies follow the mother, no matter where she goes. They stay close behind her, trying to stay in line the best they can.

Sometimes, though, the duckies get lost or fall out of line, and the mother duck must round up her duckies and keep them together in the straight path. Sometimes the mother duck might lose her way or become uncertain about the path to follow. However, if the mother turns around, she will find comfort in the fact that her duckies are right behind her.

This metaphor of the mother duck leading the duckies played out many times during my first year of teaching. One of the most memorable is when I used the song "Color Esperanza"—translated "The Color of Hope"— to inspire my students when I knew a lot of them were experiencing some rough times at home. This song is all about having hope even when things are hard. They loved the song, and they always begged me to play it for them so they could sing it. I was always able to cheer up my duckies and lead them towards more hopeful moments by playing them that song.

Then, towards the middle of the year, things got really hard for me. I was homesick, and I was feeling pretty lonely and down. Teaching was hard, and I was constantly overwhelmed with planning, grading, and completing all of my ACE assignments. I think my students could tell that I was struggling. One of the ways that my duckies would cheer me up when they knew I was overwhelmed was by asking me to play "Color Esperanza." When we listened to the song, somehow we were all inspired to keep our chins up and keep going. Even though my struggles were much different from those my students were experiencing, we all needed that same esperanza, that same hope. I needed to follow my duckies as much as they needed to follow me.

This is how the Year of the Ducks was for me. Yes, it was hard. Yes, my duckies sometimes lost their way. But I kept going through the pond and made sure I kept my duckies in line. Sometimes I, too, got lost in the pond. I wasn't sure which way to go. I wasn't sure which lessons to teach, which assignments to grade, which activities to moderate, which questions to ask. But whenever I felt lost, I would turn around and see my duckies, swimming along behind me, having faith in me when I didn't even have faith in myself. The Year of the Ducks was stressful, difficult, painful, and exhausting. But it was also a good year. It was the year when I was the Mother Ducky. ✺

Sam's Life Lessons

Walter Pruchnik  ACE 12 St. Petersburg

A couple of months into the second semester of my second year of teaching, I was very frustrated because I felt that my teaching wasn't improving, and that my students weren't learning anything. It was my lowest point in two years of teaching. I didn't think my students were learning the life lessons that I really hoped they would comprehend, even if they didn't learn the math concepts. Then one day after school, the chemistry teacher came up to me and told me this story, which reminded me that I was making a difference and helped me to remember why teaching is worth the personal suffering and frustration. She told me this story about Sam and what he said and did in her classroom that day.

Before, I continue, I need to tell you a little bit about Sam: he was about six feet, five inches tall, a lovable, fun-loving character, and had been a student in my pre-calculus class. After nearly failing the first quarter—not because he wasn't smart, but because he didn't have the background for pre-calculus—I talked with him one day after class about what it would take for him to do well. Sam took my advice and started coming to see me twice a week after school for help. His grades were improving, and it looked like Sam was probably going to get a high B for the second quarter and maybe even a B for the semester, when he told me he was going to drop the course at the semester break. He had been offered a scholarship, didn't need pre-calculus for his college admission or for his intended major, and didn't want it to hurt his GPA which could jeopardize his scholarship. Even though I was sorry to see Sam go because I thought that staying in the course could help him, I agreed, and Sam dropped my course.

Fast-forward to that spring day. In chemistry class, some of my students were complaining about what an unfair, heartless, mean teacher I was and how I wanted them all to fail. The teacher was just about to step in and put a stop to the commentary when, to her surprise, Sam turned to his classmates and said to them that they were wrong. He continued by saying that the reason they were doing poorly was because they weren't trying. He told his peers that I really did care about them and would do anything to help students succeed and learn. He also added that he never wanted to hear them disrespect me again.

For me, this story is a strong reminder of the good work that we do. Even though Sam never told me what he said to his classmates, and he didn't master the skills of higher algebra or pre-calculus, Sam knew something about being a good person and had recognized my love for him and all my students. Although I cannot claim full credit, I consider Sam one of my greatest successes as a teacher because he learned the big lessons about how to be an "honest citizen and good Christian" as our principal was fond of saying. ✪

The Courage to Dream

Beau Schweitzer ✯ ACE 7 Los Angeles

"When I call your name, tell me where you're going to college. Then you may go to recess." Thirty-six sixth graders offer stares of incomprehension. Most can't name a university. To escape, they need to stand and show one another the courage to dream.

My boys have a better chance of incarceration, girls of unwed teenage pregnancy, than of finishing high school. Sixty-five percent of area high school students drop out. Four of five adults never completed twelfth grade. But we're beating the odds. On the first day of sixth grade, my kids want recess badly enough to know where they're going to college.

Eva stands. "I'm going to UCLA." With fairytale script, she writes papers about caring for her parents and being faithful to God all her life. Her report cards blossom with As. Only her little sister knows the phone numbers of more friends by heart. I teach Eva for the next three years. She's beautiful. She has no idea her virtue enriches my love of the Virgin Mary, Cause of Our Joy.

But today she's sorrowful. Instead of going to PE, I ask Eva—now an eighth grader—to remain behind. Her cheeks mottle. She begins to sob.

"Mr. Beau, my parents fought last night. Dad threw the telephone at my step-mom. Belia and I hid in bed together, hearing all the hate I make my family feel."

"Eva, what happened?"

"My step-mom wants me to apply to Catholic school. But we can't afford it. It's really hard right now. So I'm going to Compton High. I know my sister will go to my school, too. But Belia can't go to Compton! She's smart, Mr. Beau. But nobody graduates there.

"For Belia, I asked again if I can apply to Catholic schools. It was so terrible—they were all screaming—my own family hating each other so much because of me. I hate my life. I hate the pain I cause. I'd rather die than fill my family with hurt."

Visiting a neighboring ACE community, I plod to a burrito truck for dinner. My prayers for Eva enter the twilight. Finishing my *horchata*, I take a shortcut, pocketing my Rosary to hop the St. Matthias fence. Deep in prayer, I cross Senior Square. Suddenly, a sound stalls my steps. My startled eyes lift, resting on the elevated statue of Mary. Her face perfectly overlays the moon, warm and full, in a silent spring night. Feeling Mary's gaze, I kneel in halo's glow, my heart welling with gratitude to Our Lady for bringing Eva to Jesus. One thing I know: I needn't worry for Eva anymore.

The next morning Eva arrives with an application to St. Matthias, a sudden gift from a classmate's mom. "The deadline's today but I can't fill it out at home." Eva spends her school day at my desk. Her portion finished, I complete the final details. After school, Eva's step-mom makes the submission.

Eva passes Mary's statue, taking the entrance exam while "shopping" with step-mom. Receiving one of three top scores, Eva wins the scholarship of merit. Tuition is covered! Mom can drive Eva to school. Dad sees me at Mass. This Spanish-speaker tells me Eva's future with a nod.

My sixth graders are now seniors. They wait for their names to be called, to be the courage to dream for a community gripped by fear. But graduation hurts. Stares of incomprehension linger in my students' eyes. Hector and Carlos are success stories—the prides of their families—invincible. Racing Hector's newly acquired Mustang, they reach 120 on urban streets before losing control, killing a boy on an evening walk with his mom. They die just before graduation. Twenty-four hours later, I'm on a plane to L.A.

As I walk to the funeral, I encounter Frankie's mom. We embrace. I used to drive Frankie home. He was gunned down three years ago. I ask how she's doing. Anguish surfaces as she grasps for solace. "Mr. Beau, it's better for our kids to die than have to grow up in this neighborhood."

Sitting together after the funeral on the playground of moonlit asphalt, my students and I hold one another. We ache at having more images and likenesses of God wrenched from our lives. We laugh as stories incarnate Carlos' smile and

Hector's love for homework. Carlos just finished recording his first album. The guys recall catching Hector and me watching a Veggie Tales rendition of Esther; together we studied Women of the Old Testament after school. We clean deep wounds as memories soften the TV's murderous portrayal of our friends.

Although scattered by four years and eleven Catholic schools, Hector and Carlos make us family again. And already we must say more final goodbyes. Love compels my battered students to reach beyond their brokenness to share their lone imperishable gift, the courage to dream.

"I chose UC Irvine."

"I'm going to UC Riverside."

"I chose UC Santa Barbara."

"I'm going to UC Santa Cruz."

Eva's mom approaches. She waits for translation after asking in Spanish if I have a place to stay. Now a Spanish speaker, I accept.

Eva and I talk late into the night. She's bound for UC Berkeley. Belia and Eva again share a bed, making room for me in their family. I eat breakfast with Belia, praying with her before she ventures to the SAT.

Before leaving Los Angeles, I return to Saint Malachy for a final Mass.

"Mr. Beau, you really came back."

"Jesse!"

"I'm so sorry I couldn't make the funeral. They were my best friends, but I had graduation."

"Jesse, I'm so proud of you."

"Mr. Beau, if it weren't for you, I might have been in that car." His tears fall, but Jesse fights to look me in the eye. "I start at USC in the fall." ✪

The Perfect Season

John Bacsik  ACE 11 Savannah

Imagine a kid who was too skinny to play contact sports and whose mother worried that he might get bruised during a game of two-hand touch. Now think of a kid who wore his glasses to basketball practice and just hoped not to embarrass himself when shooting free-throws. Yes, I was that child.

Fast forward fifteen years. On November 8, 2007, I held my breath as Mike Huggins, a sixth-grade student at my school, threw a 40-yard pass to Wes Witt, his teammate, with three seconds left on the clock. Wes caught the pass in the end zone as time expired, and our junior varsity football team defeated Savannah Christian to win the Savannah Parochial Athletic League Championship and complete the perfect season (9-0).

Parents, students, and faculty members rushed the field. We had pulled off an improbable victory, and the smiles on our players' faces were wider than the field they had just played upon.

One hour later, as the lights were being turned off on the field, I stopped and thought, "What if?" What if I had never been a part of ACE? I never would have known about St. James School. I never would have considered moving down to Savannah, Georgia. And I never would have been a coach of this amazing football team.

A famous coach once said, "Football is like life. It requires perseverance, self-denial, hard work, sacrifice, dedication and respect for authority." With all due respect to that coach, I think he meant to say, "Football is like the ACE program."

ACE required the perseverance to get through those nights of grading papers and planning lessons, knowing that this would benefit your students. It demanded the sacrifice of your time and your talent, helping your students, your players, and especially your community members. ACE teaches you how to respect those teachers who share their wisdom and how to earn the respect of your students.

ACE is not just about what you teach children; what you take away from this program is what the children teach you. If the only things we did in life were those we were good at, would we ever truly challenge ourselves?

I do not coach football at St. James because I was great at the sport when I was a child. For that matter, some of my own players are faster than me and they probably hit harder. Nor do I coach basketball because I could shoot gracefully. My eighth-grade girls would wear me out in a game of one-on-one.

I coach for the same reasons that I teach: it is a challenge, and it brings excitement. Every day in the classroom is like a new game in the season. You need to be prepared, you need to make good decisions, and you need to be focused in order to make yourself a better student.

As we celebrated our championship football victory at a local restaurant, a mother came up to me and thanked me for all I had done for the boys. It was ironic because I would have paid money to witness a football season that exciting, yet I had the chance to be a part of it as a coach. And someone was thanking me? This experience, for me, epitomizes the spirit of ACE: loving what you do, and being loved for what you've done.

Basketweaver

Emmeline Schoen D'Agostino ⬤ ACE 10 Tucson

In my first year of teaching, wrapped in the chaos of San Xavier Mission School fourth grade, I'd catch her in the corner of my eye, watching me shyly from the third-grade line out in the hall. She looked at me with her lips tucked between her teeth lest a smile should escape. I waited for her. I waited to sit her at a small desk before me and watch her. Just watch her. She was beautiful, with deep and lovely eyes. I knew she was aching. I knew she was broken-hearted and bore that weight with the soul of a full-grown woman. For these reasons, she was, to me, all the more precious.

***

She began making baskets in the winter. Once a week, she gathered with a small group of dedicated elders to twist yucca, beargrass, and devil's claw into further beauty. She learned slowly, as is the way, the delicate actions, the patience demanded of otherwise flighty fingers, the quiet. To my delight, she pushed her handiwork inches before my face one morning before school. She did not say a word. "Did you make this?!" A nod. "It's yours?!" A nod. "You're learning?!" A nod. "It's beautiful." A smile without teeth. I did not hear much else.

We started off the school year in August with joy amidst the sparkling heat. The commencement of the year brings a genuine love affair born of novelty and new beginnings. I floated on it for quite sometime. And she basked in it. It was peaceful. It was happy. It was wonderful. And she was my secret favorite. Come November, she began to tell me that her mother was coming home soon, moved from California to a half-way house in Tucson, close enough for weekly visits. The mother who missed first and second and third grade, as she paid her price for drug use, would soon return for the second half of fourth grade. On a tiny dry-erase board anchored on her desk, we quietly but ceremoniously counted down the days, erasing one at a time, bringing mom closer with every morning. I could not help but rejoice with her.

But if we love so, heartbreak may be in our future. And had she not loved her mother, there would be no ache. Mom spent less than one month in Tucson before finding a night lost in drinking. And then, she was back to California. We had lost her again.

***

After the second week of her basket class, she brought her work again for me to see. It had grown to three inches in diameter, twisted round and round in a coarse circle. It was as lovely as the two foot one we'd seen sold for $2,000.

***

January, after she had lost her mother again, pushed into February and March with ugliness. The child who had sat in the palm of my hand now turned her back to me, glared at me from that very same desk, stopped doing her work. I fought her, I bargained with her, I tried everything to get her back. No discipline, no threat, no punishment, no indifference, no affection, no praise could compel her. I feared her lost. One day, I kept her after school to speak to her in a final attempt. I said, "I just wish you would come back. I miss you." She scoffed and rolled her eyes. I let her walk home and resigned myself to a tearful commute.

***

At the end of March, the basket was the size of her palm. She was beginning to add devil's claw, a flash of black amidst the sun-turned yellow. When my mother and friend visited for Easter, she explained to them, in intricate detail, the process of basket-making. She talked on and on. She let them hold her masterpiece. She taught them new vocabulary. She explained her designs. When an opportunity arose to draw a picture in class, hers contained depictions of all her tools and materials. And I had noticed the quiet grace return to her. The rage was drying up. The fury was filed away with yucca and devil's claw. The anger was twisted into patterns of beauty. She was nearer herself again.

***

And then, at the beginning of April, it happened. I was at a family's house for an afternoon party. While chatting with some of the family, I noticed I had a quiet eavesdropper lurking nearby. Soon, everyone stood to go outside, and I was alone for a minute. She sat on a chair near me. "Miss Schoen," she said, "I came back." I did not understand. "Remember, you said you wished I would come back? I came back." Then she stood and left the room. I sat dumbfounded.

We do not know the effect of our words. I had forgotten my own, but she had remembered. They sat inside her for some time, and she did not forget. And despite the unfavorable reception she gave them, they stayed.

We do not live in movies and novels. We live in reality with all its mystery and imperfection. She was not perfect. She did not become an angel after that moment. She still rolls her eyes. But I know she knows. I know she knows.

***

I am here beyond any blessings I could have wished for. I am woven into baskets of pain and wonder. I am yucca, dried and bleached in the sun. I am devil's claw, black as night. She threads me through her heart and back again. She twists me with a child's deepest anger and confusion. She bends me backwards and forwards in the memory of her mother. She takes her grandmother's sadness, she takes her older brother's attempts at manhood, she takes her kid sister's tears, and weaves them with patience. She pulls them and forces them into her own design. Her fingertips are roughened, her palms sliced. She bleeds and kisses her hands. She weaves. Does she think of me? She pulls beargrass from the dry earth and shines beneath a master's guidance. She brings her progress for all to see. She has a long way to go. It does not yet reach beyond her fingertips. But it is already beautiful.

And I know, though I am but one strand, she has woven me into something beautiful.

The Price of Honesty

Justin Meyers  ACE 10 Pensacola

E Period. After lunch. Spanish I. Sophomores. Thirty-five students. Stadium-style classroom. Let's just say rambunctious was an understatement when trying to describe this class.

As a floating teacher, I had the joy of carting my classroom materials around in a hanging file folder box or "tackle box." The top of this container was see-through, filled with chalk, pencils, pens, paperclips, keys, and a dollar or two for a lunchtime snack. During one of our group work activities I noticed a group of students unusually interested in my file box. Sure enough, at the end of the activity, I noticed my dollar was missing.

Trying not to lose my cool, I sought to make this difficult situation a teachable moment. WWDD—What would Doc do?—flashed through my head. It really wasn't the dollar that bothered me; it was more an issue of respect.

I asked the students to take their seats and said I had something important to discuss with them, then feigned a moment of getting myself together. While used only twice during my two years in ACE, I found there is nothing more effective to students than a teacher on the verge of tears of disappointment. After "regaining" my composure, I explained what happened and how disappointed I was. After several murmurs of, "Just pay him!" and "Trevor, pay up!" and offers of dollars from various students, I told them I would let them settle this.

I would pass an envelope around the classroom and then go out into the hall. The person who took the dollar could return it and I would never know who did it. They could call me in when it was done, and class would continue. My students agreed this was a good plan so we carried it out. I returned to the room, opened the envelope, returned the dollar to my "tackle box" and class continued.

Fast forward two years:

I am living and working in Chicago and head down to my ACE site for an extended weekend—a chance to see teachers, friends, and students before they graduate in a few weeks. I'm standing in the hallway during afternoon announcements speaking with a group of students I used to coach. Trevor, the high school football star, comes up to us and starts chatting. We finish our conversation and all the students start walking away, when Trevor turns to me, reaches into his wallet, and says, "Hey, Mr. Meyers, I owe you this."

The dollar incident, long forgotten, instantly flashes to my mind. I smile and say thank you. He apologizes, I smile again and tell him I'm proud of him.

That was probably the best dollar I spent during all of ACE.

COMMUNITY

"Live in a manner worthy of the call you have received, with all humility and gentleness, with patience, bearing with one another through love." (Ephesians 4:1-2)

"This I command you: love one another." (John 15:17)

Blessed, Broken, and Shared: Communities of Hope

Sean McGraw, C.S.C.
Co-Founder
Alliance for Catholic Education

Fr. McGraw, together with Fr. Tim Scully, founded the ACE program in 1993. McGraw worked with Scully for the first year to create and launch the program and served as Associate Director for the following year in which forty ACE 1 teachers were placed in eight dioceses. He entered the seminary after the second summer of ACE and was ordained a Holy Cross priest in 2001. McGraw served for three years as a teacher, coach, and administrator at Notre Dame High School for Boys in Chicago, where he helped hire five ACE graduates to teach and lead the school, and was part of the original ACE Chicago community. McGraw is currently studying for a doctorate in Comparative Politics at Harvard University and has recently returned from sixteen months in Ireland as a Fulbright Scholar-in-Residence, where he conducted research for his dissertation. McGraw has served as a spiritual mentor and guide for the Boston and Dublin ACE Fellowship communities during his stays in those cities and remains part of the ACE Advisory Board.

One of the most spectacular miracles in the Gospels is the feeding of the five thousand. After days of Jesus' teaching and healing and leading the crowds, the disciples realize the people are hungry and far from any towns. The disciples have nothing to offer them—or so they think—until a small child steps forward with five loaves and two fish. That's all Jesus needs—some fragments of food—this is enough. What follows are the simple actions we have come to know so well: Jesus takes the bread, blesses it, breaks it, and then shares it with the disciples, who in turn, share the food with the multitudes. Not only does Jesus take what little they have and multiply it, but he ensures that they are the ones who feed each other and, ultimately, the five thousand. And there is enough left over to fill twelve wicker baskets.

The multiplication of the loaves can, in many ways, represent the Community Pillar in ACE. Those called to do ACE have already witnessed and been inspired by Jesus' teaching and healing and have been brought together to share their gifts in their respective classrooms, schools, parish communities, and dioceses. The primary lesson we have learned from the Gospels and the Christian experience over time is that our journey with God is not one to be undertaken alone. Rather, the Christian experience is fundamentally a communal one.

In ACE we have discovered that for young people to survive the challenges of the first years of teaching and to endure doubts, hungers, and failures, as well as to celebrate joys, small victories, and miracles, they must live and work and share their lives together, and be surrounded by people who support them in their mission. The very act of living, working, praying, eating, and playing together offers these often tired and worn-out servants an opportunity to be fed by one another—and Jesus—and to be rejuvenated for their ongoing service to others. At different moments, each community member is the one who has the fragments to share, when others have nothing left to give. It is this sharing and commitment to one another that Jesus takes, blesses, and gives to the ACE teachers so that they may be fed, and in turn, can feed those they are called to serve.

Each community in ACE takes on its own set of living conditions and schedule of communal meals, prayers, social nights, retreats, and other activities. From former convents to apartments to old Southern homes; from meals every night to once per week; from carpooling an hour to school to walking next door; from inserting themselves into welcoming communities filled with young people and families to being the only young Catholic adults within an hour; from praying each day together to praying each day that their housemates don't drive them nuts; the contrast of communal living in ACE is endless. Still, at the core of each community experience, is an invitation to feed others, to be fed by them as well, and to place Jesus at the center of our lives.

Whereas the classroom experience is what draws all of us together and stretches us to discover our gifts and limitations, the community experience can be equally as formative and challenging. We learn that, as Christian leaders, we cannot just pour everything into our work and then be a completely different person and have a completely different outlook outside the walls of our classrooms. Ultimately, as Christian leaders who have seen and done so much, we know that we must be present to others in all that we do. The ACE community experience thrusts this upon each teacher and forces him or her to give until it hurts. Through communal living in ACE we develop an ability to be open to the needs of the people with whom we live and work, even though they may be the last persons we would have chosen to share this work and journey.

The simple lessons learned in community paved the way for better teaching and for becoming a better person. As Christian Dallavis once remarked about community life in ACE, one learned to know when to tease the housemates you live with and when to leave them alone; or one learned to ask for help in simple matters like how to cook but also to ask for help in much more difficult situations like how to walk with a twelve-year-old who lost a parent. In the end, it is the culmination of these experiences that shape us and feed us and ultimately prepare us to take these blessed fragments that Jesus has given us and to share them with others so they too can be fed.

Yet, this is not just about two years in ACE. Just like the disciples who only had two or three years with Jesus, but went on to walk with Jesus for the rest of their lives creating new communities, so too, ACE teachers carry their experiences with them along their life journeys. Simple things, like hearing one's class song— from ACE 3's "I Want You to Want Me" to ACE 11's "Don't Stop Believing"— can conjure up the memories of a crazy group of young people who got each other through challenging times by believing in one another, and this provides strength and encouragement for current challenges. The ACE community experiences are only the beginning of lives shared together to strengthen us to live the Gospel.

One can think about the three ACE 1 graduates who traveled around the world for a year only to knock on Katie (Floyd) Donnino's (ACE 1) doorstep years later in Washington, DC, because they knew they had a home there. Or think about the hundreds of ACE teachers who showed up at Tim Williamson's (ACE 3) funeral and continue to wear a rubber band around their wrist to recall Tim's goodness and willingness to do whatever his friends needed. Or the countless "ACE Weddings" there have been, including two of the editors of this volume, who found in their ACE community a soul mate with whom they wanted to share, sacramentally, the rest of their lives. The stories and ways in which ACE teachers continue to be fed by the people with whom they taught and lived with those years ago is infinite.

What follows, then, is a collection of these stories from ACE teachers about the homes they lived in, the people that picked them up when they were down, and the places that led them to discover themselves anew as people of faith and service. These present-day disciples have learned and been fed by Jesus, and are now sharing the fruits of this multiplication with those in need. May these stories remind us of the need to share our journey of faith and service with others and to allow God to use these relationships to spread the Good News and to build up the Church, of which we all have been called to be leaders. In the end, Christ multiplies what little we have, gives it to us to share with others, and there is plenty left over once all have had their fill. For this great and ongoing source of life, we give deep thanks.

What Remains

Dave Devine  ACE 1 Baton Rouge

I probably can't give you what you want.

You are likely expecting something neat and cogent and concise, and all I have to offer is the sprawling messiness of memory. You are eager to hear—no doubt—about the pioneering spirit of the initial class of ACE teachers, the plucky determination of forty fresh faces on their way to new and welcome challenges, and all I seem to recall is uncertainty and confusion mixed with measured optimism. A roomful of people with more questions than answers. A program planned on a paper napkin. An ambitious vision crammed into the corner of a disheveled office. A persistent priest with hair that was constantly akimbo. A terrain that shifted daily beneath our feet, sometimes seismically.

I'd like to tell you that we dove into rigorous classes and absorbed a stimulating curriculum with abandon, but that would be misleading. The classes we attended that first summer felt improvised, variable, made up weekly as we went along. Which was appropriate training—soon many of us would be teaching classes which we'd improvise, make up, vary as we went along. Still, it didn't exactly feel like innovation back then, and it certainly didn't feel like we were on the cusp of some glorious movement in Catholic education. It felt like all things that are difficult and daunting when you're buried in the midst of them. It felt like something more than we were meant to handle.

And I'm not sure that's what you want to hear about.

You want to hear about inspiring lesson plans and altered lives and compelling community dinners, and I want to tell you about playing soccer in the pouring rain and lives that never changed and grilled cheese sandwiches burnt so badly we laughed until we cried. You want to hear about Defining Moments and Lasting

Impacts, and I want to tell you about a daiquiri shop that drowned the memories of a wasted week, a buckled tabletop covered with more crawfish than you've ever seen, a Sunday night when we abandoned our half-completed progress reports to drive to New Orleans and watch a man play a saxophone standing on his head.

I want to tell you about the rest of that night, barreling home through a hundred pitch-black miles of bayou to Baton Rouge and staying up until dawn grading backlogged essays and still failing to finish and arriving at a faculty inservice three hours late and sheepishly submitting the slipshod reports and promptly retreating home to sleep for three more fitful hours and then enduring, the next day, a terse meeting with a disapproving Vice Principal filled with uncomfortable silences and averted glances.

I want to tell you that nearly fourteen years later I fail to remember a word of that Vice Principal's reprimand, but the wailing saxophone in that smoky blues club?

Jesus, it comes back to me.

And really, that's the way it is with all of it—this mangled warp and weft of memory. Every time I attempt to mine a thread of something worth telling, a stubborn scrap of some other story inevitably emerges. Something contrarian and inchoate and unexpected. A summer night on campus before we ever started teaching, when the sprinklers were shushing out on the quad and the lake was beckoning with its cool dark waters and the night was still bursting with possibility. Or a wood-paneled station wagon crammed with more people than it should have safely held. Or an off-campus bar crowded with future teachers dancing and spilling beer on each other to the beat of "Paradise by the Dashboard Light." Or a student weeping in a quiet courtyard. Or a student laughing in detention. Or a student rolling up a sweatshirt sleeve to reveal a forearm etched with shallow razor cuts. Or a gymnasium maze of tri-fold display boards adorned with sloppy social studies projects. Or a rusted stadium pressbox looming over a Friday night football game. Or a sun-splashed afternoon on a dirt road in Louisiana, running with an all-White cross country team while a laughing, pointing busload of Black children rumbles past. Having no idea what that means or why it stays with me, but just knowing that it does. Knowing that it is seared into memory, like so many other things from those two years.

But that's probably not what you want to hear.

Community

You want to hear the timeless stories I recount whenever someone asks about my ACE experience, and I want to tell you the stories I've never shared with anyone. Stories of shame and embarrassment and anger. The day I whistled a handful of chalk over the startled heads of a class of distracted students. The fourteen-year-old boy I nearly punched in sheer frustration. The stack of essays and quizzes, thick as two city phone books, I tossed in the trash instead of grading. The Friday afternoon I gently closed the classroom door after the final student had left, sat down at my desk, took off my glasses, and wept in desperation.

I want to tell you about the December day I walked into our community apartment to find a carved pumpkin, which had been rotting on the floor in neglect since Halloween, riddled with darts buried to their shafts in the jack-o-lantern's face. How I took one look at my roommate, who was halfway through grading a pile of journals he'd been avoiding since October, then glanced at the empty dartboard, and knew exactly what had happened. And why. And how we exchanged grim nods and set jaws and then I retreated to my bedroom and started on my own pile of journals.

But maybe that's not what you want to hear. Even though stories of frailty are more interesting and honest, stories of strength sell books and make for rousing movie trailers.

With that in mind, here's a movie trailer:

There were stunning successes those first two years. There were improbable Teacher of the Year trophies and lives that really were altered and students who absorbed more than they had any business learning in our cobbled-together classrooms. There were innovative lessons and heroic levels of dedication and college graduates finding lifelong vocations in a field they never imagined entering. In the fourteen years since, there have been thousands of children served and national awards and an ever-expanding program that stretches across the nation. There are students of former ACE teachers who are themselves now teaching, which is no small thing.

But there is also this: On a random Tuesday morning I open my laptop and go on-line to find a string of casual, pointless e-mails occupying my in-box, and copied on the exchange are almost all of the forty teachers who started together that first year of ACE. The initial e-mail was not an ACE reunion notice or a request from Notre Dame's alumni office that happened to be targeted at our class; it was a short, senseless sarcastic note sent to nearly forty friends scattered around the country on a random Tuesday morning, almost fourteen years later.

I've lost contact with almost all of my high school friends. I'm in touch with no more than a handful of acquaintances from college. But on any given day, more than a decade after entering the ACE program with a collection of people I'd mostly never met, I can open my e-mail account and find conversations that pick up as if we were still sitting in a room together in Sorin Hall.

I collaborated on a screenplay with one of these classmates. I drove the length of Australia in a rented van with another. I have stood in their weddings and cradled their children and fielded their phone calls in the middle of the night. I have shed more tears and downed more beers in their collective presence than I care to recall. I can't tell you why these friendships have held when others haven't, just as I can't tell you why a busload of Black children on a back road in Louisiana is seared into my mind.

It just is.

If you're looking for a story, I'm afraid you've come to the wrong place. All I have to offer is a heaving, swirling, unreliable tapestry of memories. A collection of summer nights and sweatshirt sleeves and saxophone players. A table piled high with crawfish and a chaotic, clamoring classroom. Friday afternoon tears and Tuesday morning e-mails that make me roar with laughter.

Fourteen years later, that's what remains.

Chicken Italiano

Molly (Davis) Hahn  ACE 3 Tulsa

I stand at my kitchen counter adding spices to a mixture that will become the breading on a chicken breast, not needing to check the recipe for my husband's favorite Italian chicken. He has told me that because it was the entrée I made the first time I ever cooked for him, he will always call it his favorite. Yet, I will always make it with a bit of nostalgia for my time in Tulsa, Oklahoma, because the recipe came from my housemate, Kevin Langell, who got it from his mother.

It's the butter dripping, really. That's what you smell when the chicken is cooking, and in those days, our novice chef skills caused all of us to think chicken with handmade breading was just about the most gourmet meal we could manage. Besides that, we couldn't afford chicken for every meal from our joint checking account, so it was a special occasion when Kevin made this chicken. Normally he would serve it over rice that came from an economy-sized container, and if we were really lucky, we would also get garlic bread and a green salad.

Our dinners together were what really strengthened our community because we had an unusual circumstance: the men lived in a separate house from the women. Though I was extremely disappointed at the time because we didn't have the traditional community feel, I know that we ate together more often than others, and that dinner table served for our collective growth.

We took turns cooking, and our recipes were not always a success like the Italian chicken. In fact, there were definitely some inedible dishes created on experimental basis, and our palates varied widely enough to create disagreements about the menu.

Yet, something happened as we ate that went beyond the food on the table. We heard about all of the successes and failures as teachers and coaches, and we shared stories from each of our hometowns and childhood traditions. Like a family, I remember both laughter and frustrated feelings at that dinner table. While our traditional blessing before each meal probably should have led to what Fr. Scully often calls "breaking bread," our dinner table often contained some not-so-holy conversation that ranged from the antics of our students to personal details that would be better not repeated in writing. We began as strangers eating food together, and we left two years later with a community bond through the sharing of meals.

I realize today that the dinner ritual is one that I savor for a couple of reasons. First, I found out that I really like to cook. Before ACE, I had never tried to cook for myself. In the years since, I have taken lessons from my mom and my grandmother and learned the value of homemade recipes. I love figuring out what combinations of spices complement each other, and I experiment with new dishes as often as I can. I still make many of the recipes we made in ACE, but my repertoire is far greater now.

More importantly, though, is the ritual of the dinner itself: the setting of the table, the blessing, the sharing of dishes. My parents always made sure that my brothers and I ate dinner together with a blessing, and now in all of the chaos of daily life, my husband and I are attempting to do the same as often as we can. It's unrealistic to think it can happen every night, but as we prepare to welcome our first baby into the world, we intend to instill in this child, and all our children, the importance of sharing meals together. Secretly, I think it gives him motive to ask me to make Italian chicken more often.

We Can Do That

Michael Faggella-Luby ✪ ACE 5 Jacksonville

Under the orange neon lights of the AutoZone sign, we stared across the open hood of the '83 Oldsmobile Cutlass Ciera. The tow truck drove away into the warm summer night leaving our broken down car behind. In disbelief, Dave's final words to the driver echoed in my ears: "We can do that." We can do that! Was Dave crazy? The driver had just explained to us that Elsje's car needed a new alternator and that we could buy one inside the store. He had apologized that he couldn't stay to help us, but since Dave had a few tools, he thought we would be fine changing the alternator ourselves. Ourselves! Perhaps the driver was unaware of several key points: (1) the "tools" to which he referred were a Christmas gift from Dave's mother and had never actually been out of the box, (2) I had not processed anything in his uninterrupted seven-minute, jargon-filled explanation of how to complete the procedure after he used the phrase, "don't forget or it might blow up," and (3) the automotive expertise among the three of us centered on reminding each other periodically to get an oil change at Jiffy Lube every 3,000 or so miles. How were we going to do this?

The trip had started with promise and hope. Elsje, Dave, and I had formed a caravan of three cars to drive the thousand miles from our house in Jacksonville, Florida to South Bend. Our school year in the Diocese of St. Augustine had ended on Friday, so we had two days to get to Notre Dame before classes for our second ACE summer began the following Monday. We were a motley crew at best. Dave drove a 1993 Civic he had purchased from a former ACEr, and was using a hockey stick propped under his arm to regulate his speed as a homemade cruise control. He never could get it quite right and so while Elsje and I stayed together, his car was constantly five miles ahead or five miles behind. Elsje's car was a gift to the ACE house arranged by our superintendent, Pat Tierney, and had made it possible for many of us to get to work. The Oldsmobile had seen a lot of living as evidenced by the scrapes, dents, and rust spots on its faded baby-blue exterior. I recall that Elsje had already had to have the car jumped several times. In fact, part of the purpose of our caravan was to make sure that we nursed the car to Notre Dame in one piece. In the days before everyone had cell phones, I feared we would never be able to get there as a group. So we left palm trees behind, crossed through the Appalachian Mountains, and entered the unending sky and plains of the Midwest. The first day of travel passed without incident. The next day, our luck ran out.

As we prepared to leave on the second morning, we discovered that Elsje's car would not start. Demonstrating the full extent of our knowledge of cars, we hooked her car up to mine for a "jump," by following the step-by-step directions attached to the cables by a note card. Even with the directions, we used the phrase, "I don't know, what do you think?" a little too often. The need to jump the car surfaced twice over the next two hundred miles until we pulled into a Travelers gas station in Seymour, Indiana, where the car seemed to gasp its final breath. A quick call and three-hour wait for a AAA tow truck later and we were standing in the AutoZone parking lot alone. Our only chance to make it to Notre Dame in time for classes on Monday was to change the alternator ourselves because the nearest garage could not have the car fixed earlier than Wednesday morning. How were we going to do this?

The answer was pretty simple: We were going to do it together. In what became known in our house as the incident of "Mike and the Mechanics," we carefully reconstructed what the driver had told us—shared memory is wonderful—and when the new alternator didn't exactly line up with the existing supports, we used a little creative problem solving to get the car back on the road for the final push to ND.

I will argue with anyone that no three Domers have ever been so happy to see campus as we were when we pulled up to the dorms. Elsje hugged Dave and me and we shared a quiet moment. We had made it together, the same way we had made it through our first year, and the same way we would make it through the next. It is difficult to put into words what happened on that trip, but the trust that we had developed as community members facing the challenges of the classroom had allowed us to reach beyond our individual limitations. It is said that necessity is the mother of invention. In our case, I think that necessity brought out the best in each of us, allowing us to collectively solve our problem. There were several times that we each wanted to give up, or admit that it could not be done and call it quits. But because we had the safety of each other, we were willing to take the risks, to share what we had learned, to draw upon the strengths of others in our time of crisis.

Margaret Mead tells us to never doubt that a small group of thoughtful, committed citizens can change the world. While we were not changing the world—it was just an alternator—I like to think that we were practicing and developing the strategies and strengths that will help each of us to change the world. In our collaboration, we embodied the spirit of the ACE program: A hope in the possibility that if we take the very best of each of us and put these gifts to work in collaboration with others, we can improve the lives of all children, their families, and their schools through Catholic education. ACE draws upon our individual desires to better our world and helps to shape each of us by providing countless opportunities to grow through our teaching, community, and faith. Change the world? We can do that.

The Room That Boxes Built

Eric Amato  ACE 8 Los Angeles

It all started in year one of ACE—the big move. I drove from Chicago to Los Angeles with my best friend. The over two thousand mile trip was a smooth one except for one detail. We arrived at the new ACE house and didn't have keys to get in. Fortunately, my roommates arrived shortly after, and from that first day our lives quickly fell into a normal routine, filled with laughter, highs and lows, and comic relief.

Our routine, however, was not considered normal by most. The six of us lived in a three-bedroom house, and because we made one room into a computer/work room, we were left with three adults to each bedroom. Not your typical living situation by anyone's standards, but we managed to make it work.

The girls' room was attached to the bathroom and was bigger, but not by much. The guys' room was much too small for any three individuals—save kindergarteners—to comfortably enjoy. I can recall many nights where I would kick my roommate's alarm clock off the nightstand and roll over to snuggle with my other roommate. It was definitely a year to get to know one another; personal space was out the window.

The second year began with another move. This time, it was just a few miles away on the campus of one of our ACE schools. We were all excited about getting our own rooms. Well, we were close to getting our own rooms. There were 5 rooms and 6 people. We knew we had to decide who was going to share a room, but everyone wanted his own space after the cramped quarters our first year.

I spoke up and offered to stay in the garage. It had four walls and a concrete floor. What more could anyone want after the trials of our first living situation? The only problem was that it was not very private, being a garage and all. So what does a history major with no mechanical ability do? Create a wall of boxes. I took all the moving boxes in the house, along with a few refrigerator boxes, and made a wall that separated the garage in two and allowed for some privacy. I also picked up some cheap mismatched carpet and carpeted the floor. It wasn't bad. I might even venture to say that I liked it.

My bedroom in the garage stayed relatively warm throughout the year, and we even got to show off my fine workmanship when Father Scully came to visit our house. He had come to celebrate Thanksgiving Mass, and we thought it would be nice to give him a tour of our new house. He took one look at the room, gave a wry smile and said, "I love it! Does your mom know about this?"

I eventually told her. ✪

Running on Empty

Michael Downs  ACE 7 Austin

Austin, Texas, is a dangerous place to train for a marathon. Not just because the thermometer bubbles above 100. Not just because draught conditions occasionally limit water availability. Not just because Lance Armstrong turned people off jogging and onto bikes. The reason Austin is a dangerous place to train for a marathon, in my experience, is the prevalence of poisonous spiders and the toll they can take on a runner with just one bite.

Thirty-six ACE teachers, including all three of my housemates, were training around the country to run 26.2 miles, raise money for the poorest ACE school, and create what has become an annual celebration of running and revelry. Apparently the ACE 7 class helped establish a tradition: When your cohort reaches a state of communal exhaustion in the classroom, it's time to "take a break" by running 26.2 miles. Of this ambitious group, I emerged, foolishly, as the only one training for a time, not just for fun.

I was three months into a rigorous training program and determined to run under three hours, fifteen minutes. I ran in the mornings and evenings. I ignored my body's pleas for more food and sleep. Eventually, however, I could not jog away a strange swelling that began in my foot before spreading to my ankle and leg. The Montana in me figured it was a sprained ankle and decided to tough it out, run it out, stick it out. As my jog devolved into a walk, my walk into a limp, my P.E. teaching into pathetic sideline whistle-blowing, I tried not to admit the pain that everyone else could see.

Somehow word spread to my mom that I was struggling, and she called my school's secretaries to request that they not let her son leave campus until he had called a doctor. Janet and Juanita, my surrogate mothers in Austin, gladly agreed.

They were waiting for me after the final bell, one with arms crossed in front of the exit gate, the other with phone extended. Luckily, the doctor they connected me to, our principal's sister, agreed to meet me immediately in her hospital hallway between patients. After one gruesome glimpse at my leg, she diagnosed me with severe cellulitis, the result of a sizeable spider bite on the back of my calf. If I had waited a few more weeks, she scorned, it could have resulted in amputation. A marathon time of 3:15 would have really been tough on one leg.

She prescribed some antibiotics and ordered me to do no physical exercise for at least two weeks.

"Two weeks?" I calculated.

"Yes," she said, "absolutely nothing for two weeks. And drink a lot of water; the medication will make you dry as a bone."

I agreed to follow the doctor's orders, then turned and limped away, glancing at a calendar on the wall. The marathon was exactly two weeks away.

After the doctor-prescribed hiatus, I showed up at the starting line of the Los Angeles marathon rusty, but ready to go. Unfortunately, a bomb scare delayed the departure until 10 a.m. and the heat grew with each passing minute. After the starting gun and a slow first two miles of chaos, I found my groove of the previous months. This could be three hours of hell, I figured, but the faster I ran, the faster it would be over. ACErs in the race for the right reasons—community, laughter, and camaraderie—cheered the wobbly warrior on to his goal.

At mile twenty, the pain wasn't bothering me anymore. Instead, my head had become completely loopy and I was having a hard time focusing. The faster I ran, the faster this would be over. The blur of the mile 22 marker was the last thing I remember seeing before drifting completely out of focus, out of the race, and into a complicated near-death experience. Three-and-a-half hours later a nurse wiggled me awake in an L.A. hospital, where beds were full of marathon runners who had too much heat and too little water. The man next to me was a Kenyan from the lead pack. He winked and gave me a thumbs-up as I tried to orient myself.

After diagnosing me with heat exhaustion and severe dehydration, probably compounded by the cellulitis medication and my reluctance to stop for water for fear of wasting time, the nurse sent me on my way. A taxi dropped me off in the ACE meet-up spot, but all the other runners were gone. The glow of my mystical experience faded like the sun, and I realized my predicament: sweaty, injured, alone, and stranded in downtown Los Angeles. After wandering the streets of downtown

L.A., I was approached by a woman.

"Honey, you look like you could use a warm fuzzy."

"Yes, I could."

After hearing about my story and the other ACE marathoners, she proudly confessed that she was a Baptist school teacher who knew just where to take me. She walked me to the downtown chapel, where a group of religious marathoners—nuns, priests, and seminarians—were having a post-race party.

"Y'all, this Catholic boy has lost his friends. Can you help him out?"

As they warmly welcomed me in, the angel from the street offered me all the money she had—which I declined—and disappeared into the night. While my new friends in the "Running for Vocations" t-shirts offered me snacks, I borrowed a cell phone to track everyone else down.

In the meantime, the other ACE runners and a host of family and friends had gathered at the house of a prominent donor to share stories of the race that everyone had finished. Everyone, that is, except the guy who was supposed to be the first finisher. Through a series of phone calls and prayers, my ACE 7 brothers finally found me. Beau Schweitzer, Patrick Burns, Patrick Fennessey, and Tim O'Rourke eventually arrived at the downtown chapel to escort me back to the after-party.

When I arrived, the entire crowd of runners forgot their own bruised toenails and weary legs to welcome and embrace their fallen friend. Fr. Scully escorted me to a room where I could shower and change. When I returned to the common space, he and the group had just begun a living room liturgy. I turned to a friend and whispered through parched lips words borrowed from Jesus in that day's Gospel reading, as he spoke to a Samaritan woman after his own tiring trek: "Give me a drink of water." As we celebrated Mass and the falling and rising of the grueling recent days and months, I reveled in the joy of being found, filled, and welcomed home without ever crossing the finish line.

Oh, the Places You'll Go!

Phil Autrey  ACE 2 Charlotte

Congratulations!
Today is your day.
You're part of ACE 2,
Now get on your way!

To teach in the South,
Serve the Church,
Is your charge;
Working in schools,
Both small and large.

In Charlotte on Elm Lane,
Jason and Lee had the scoop.
Then after awhile,
Phil joined the Loop.
Both Sarahs shopped weekly,
At Bi-Lo much cheaper;
Snubbing the luxuries,
Of TajMa Teeter.
Paying the rent
Wasn't always a cinch.
But selling concessions
Came through in a pinch.

Then there was Kevin,
Mr. Biceps, girls winking,
Many weekends he'd hit the
Slopes and go skiing.

In Columbia four more
Taught their students with care,
Just don't wake the, um, neighbors
It wouldn't be fair.
After two years,
Three moved away.
But Cabs fell in love,
And is still there today.

In Charleston another
Quartet there resided.
Three on their chores
Always seemed undecided.
Many nights out for dinner
To Wild Wings they'd go cruisin',
And along for the ride,
Was Mia's pal Susan.

The Spirit of ACE

On St. Patrick's Day,
The river was always dyed green
In Savannah the host
Of some interesting scenes.
The town squares were covered
All over with ivy,
While Kristen and Andrew
Taught on the island of Tybee.

Down I-95,
There existed a nunnery
Where Jax teachers lived
Who could throw a great party.
Don't be fooled by this trio
No ifs ands or maybes–
Erin was quick to say,
"Come and get it baby."

Pensacola the next stop
As this trip heads due west,
Where five teachers' skills
Were put to the test.
It's said all we need
Is learned by first grade,
What a challenge for Christine
Those six-year-olds made.

In Montgomery once weekly,
At the Hills' they would dine;
A mentor named Doc
Made these kids toe the line.
So now up at ND,
He works with the teachers;
Just don't try to tell him
Lessons plans are optional features.

In Mobile, the tall man
Was Dan with a plan,
To transport ACE teachers
In the Little Flower Van.
Another split household
Of ACE 1 and 2,
But it was when ACE 3 came to town
That love would shine through.
Kate and Theo would marry
Years down the road,
But they weren't the first
ACE romance to unfold.

Enter the Gulf Coast—
A community of six.
Initial reactions
Were "Look at this mix!"
But after two years,
What a tight group instead,
With Zack and Laura
The first housemates to wed.

Mr. President and four others
Landed in Jackson.
Their old Southern home
Was not without action.
A ball player, two Jens
and the Irish McGuire–
Mississippi wouldn't be the same
By the time they'd retire.

Louisiana was spotted
With many ACE I,
But only our Cheryl
Worked with Bayou sons.

Community

In Baton Rouge
Civics lessons to teach,
Paving the way
For her commencement speech.

For miles and miles,
Not another site to be seen.
Lest we forget
The OKC team.
Each night these three worked
Until it got late,
To teach at their schools
In the Sooner state.

Now we're all grown up
and wondering, "When did we rest
between planning our lessons
and grading those tests?"
With the help of our housemates,
Always there by our side,
Providing support when we laughed
and we cried.

And many inspired us from far away–
Joe Pa and Blaine with a kind word to say.
Over two summers we learned from the
best;
A Portland degree on our walls now
does rest.

To recount all our tales
Would take quite some time.
So a couple of updates
To finish this rhyme.

While Nasser in Chicago puts bad guys
away,
Kevin runs the ER saving the day.
Tom and Pat began to teach
At Andrew's alma mater,
Bishop Dunne now an ACE hub
It couldn't be hotter.
Their time in Big D was planned for one
year–
Ten classes later, now husbands and
fathers, still there.
The same goes for Dirk,
Remaining in Charleston.
While Cheryl and Dan in Portland
Search for Barb Munson.

The ACE family grows,
More and more every year.
More weddings and babies
Abound to give cheer.
The newest to join us
Is Aimee's girl Devin.
Might she be a teacher
In ACE 37?

Oh the places you'll go
Oh the places we went
I can't say enough of those two years we
spent.

The Thursday of The Beast

Colleen Moak Ringa  ACE 9 Austin

ACE 9 Austin was a near-perfect community, creating a home environment that would make even the Cleavers jealous. We prayed with and for each other in the morning before we left for school, had four official community dinners together a week, three unofficial ones many other weeks, carpooled to school, spent sickening amounts of time together, and still managed to get along famously. Other than Mark's tendency to chew with his mouth open, we never had anything to complain about at the community problem-solving meetings at the December Retreat. Heck, our second year we didn't even have a moderator, but instead led each other in a praise-fest that led us to tears of mutual admiration. While several communities had their fair share of adversity, Dan, Mark, Melissa, and I happily supported one another throughout our ACE experience. We faced no challenges to our strength and courage as a community and felt as mighty as oxen after surviving all of our first and most of our second years of teaching, until The Beast decided to pay a visit to our storybook ACE community.

During the spring of our second year, construction began on a Wal-Mart just down the road from our house. While I am sure that the communities that followed us in Austin enjoyed its convenience and its alleged low prices, we felt no love for the new shopping venue. Rather, in our home on Texas Oaks Drive, we were unhappily saddled with rodents whose homes were being evacuated and who were in need of a place to lay their disease-infested heads. Gross.

At first, the problem was merely in our walls, with our guests' scurrying and gnawing as the only sign of their presence. This audible announcement of their desire to be a part of our community was soon followed by visuals—sightings, nibblings, and droppings—that let us know we were in for a fight. Glue traps did the trick at first, and our catch-and-release program was quite generous given the filthy nature of our furry foes. Then came the ROUS (Rodent of Unusual Size) and the corresponding devastation to our home resulting from our attempts to trap it.

I don't know what this gigantic rat, henceforth referred to as The Beast, was doing in our house, or how it made its way all the way to Austin, Texas, from the New York City subway system. What I do know is that there is nothing quite as frightening as being awakened by something of its size and general icky-ness in the middle of the night. Memory does not serve me well enough to recall whose room it wriggled into, but all of us were awake before long.

We spent the better part of three hours in the middle of that Thursday night tearing apart our house in an effort to catch The Beast. Melissa was our captain, standing atop a chair with a broom and a flashlight as if she could stun The Beast with bright light and bat it away if it ever leapt towards her. Mark was clad in football receiver's gloves as if we would engage in a little tossing of the old rat skin at the adventure's end. Dan and I were each armed, but under-protected when compared with our partners in crime. It was time to capture The Beast.

Too large to fit in any trap conceived by man, or at least any sold at the local grocery store, we were forced to attempt to capture it in cardboard boxes. Furniture was overturned, pizza-box barricades were constructed, lamps were broken, major appliances were moved, and shrieks of laughter and disgust punctuated the night. Our neighbors who previously knew us as the bunch that never mowed their lawn probably came up with many more colorful descriptors for us that night.

After a long battle against a stealthy adversary, we at last succeeded in cornering and trapping The Beast and victory and peace were ours once again. We were humane enough to continue our tradition of setting our captives free, but did so by throwing The Beast into a dumpster many miles away from our house and still inside its cardboard prison. We reasoned that if it could gnaw its way through our walls, it was likely able to overcome the pithy obstacles with which it was presented. That is what we tell ourselves to rid ourselves of any inklings of guilt, anyway. Compassion for God's creation went out the window at 3 a.m.

Dan, Mark, Melissa, and I had had many conversations leading up to that night about the many jobs we did as teachers and as ACE community members. We fancied ourselves instructors, coaches, counselors, nurses, advisers, peacemakers, and chauffeurs to name a few, but it wasn't until the Thursday of The Beast that we discovered within us the power of fearless exterminators as well.

Car Troubles

Heidi Eppich Druist ⬤ ACE 7 Tulsa

Pat Fennessy and I both taught at Saints Peter and Paul Catholic School, on Tulsa's north side. He had been assigned to the sixth-grade class, and I was teaching second graders. Our school and parish were a bright spot in an otherwise neglected neighborhood.

Neither Pat nor I owned a car that first ACE year. Our principal told us not to worry, that the Diocese of Tulsa would provide us with some sort of transportation to our school site. One very hot August afternoon, a couple of days before school would be in session, John Kraus, the principal at Saints Peter and Paul School, told us that he had good news. A car would be donated to our community in a matter of weeks, and until that time, we had two options: driving Old Red or New Yellow. I looked at Pat, we laughed, and asked what that meant. Old Red, it turned out, was a red pick-up, the school's maintenance vehicle. New Yellow? That was the school bus!

We finally did receive a car a few weeks later, and Pat and I were extremely grateful. To say that this car needed work, however, would be the understatement of the year. The car was a brown, twenty-year-old Buick Park Avenue. The first time that I got in, I realized that the driver's seat was stuck permanently in the reclined position. I had to sit straight up, hunched over the steering wheel like an old lady, just to drive it. The radio, we soon learned, had a mind of its own. We would be listening to music on the way to school, and suddenly, the volume would turn up full blast, blaring the songs for a few seconds. Then, just as randomly, it would become barely audible.

One day the speedometer stopped working. I learned to drive with the flow of traffic after that. Flat tires, leaking radiators, and brakes failing became part of our everyday life. But probably the greatest challenge of that car was figuring out how to manage the "engine surge points," as one mechanic pointed out to me. One cold morning in January, the Buick literally drove Pat and me to school. The engine accelerated by itself. I would have my foot completely off the gas, and yet, we'd continue to move along the road, faster and faster, until the speed peaked at around forty-five miles per hour. Stoplights were the worst. I had to floor the brake, just to prevent the car from hopping forward when I needed it to stop. You might surmise that my right leg received quite a workout on the way to school!

Looking back, I am amazed that the Buick actually lasted through the two-year ACE experience. No one ever bothered it, that was for sure. Its missing hubcaps and faded paint job suggested more of an abandoned vehicle than a functioning car. Pat proposed that we roll it into the Arkansas River, when we departed from Tulsa, which we ultimately decided not to do. But through the ups and downs, "Brownie" was there for us, providing what we needed, which was transportation to school.

My Own Mission in Education

Scott Reis  ACE 5 Charlotte

When I think of my ACE experience and how it has shaped my life, I am grateful to say that is has not just defined my career, but it has provided me with a mission and passion for what I do. I am in my tenth year of teaching, and it is really hard to fathom that eight years have passed since my time in ACE!

When I first heard about ACE, I was an engineering major at The University of Portland who was trying to decide what career path to take after realizing that engineering was not for me. I switched my major to mathematics, knowing I would be marketable in the field of education and in the corporate world. I never seriously thought about teaching as a career until I heard about the ACE program and my friend Tanya Wangsmo, ACE 2, told me about her experience. I knew I wanted to do some sort of service program after college and I liked the idea of living in a different part of the country and "testing out" teaching for two years. I remember telling myself that if I didn't like teaching, at least I would have experienced living in a new city, made a difference in the lives of some students, and earned a Master's degree. So I went into it with an open mind, ready to make some new friends and enjoy my summers at Notre Dame as much as possible.

I remember that first summer and how much was crammed into a mere two months: student teaching, lots of classes, studying, community bonding time, socializing, Mass, retreats, and minimal sleep. We were always tired and getting up early to student teach was not easy. My summer roommate and resident comedian, John Schoenig, had a phrase that summed up our first summer: "Something's gotta give!" He would say that whenever we had to just laugh at the seemingly impossible workload they heaped upon us. I honestly do not know how we got through that summer. We were the guinea pigs of the new

M.Ed. program from Notre Dame as the first four ACE classes received their degree from The University of Portland, and I think they wanted to push us to the breaking point to prove that this was a serious program and not just a fun service experience. On top of that, we all had to do this huge portfolio project, mostly during the second year, that consisted of thirty different "artifacts" of our teaching that had to meet these different standards, including INTASC, AYA, and others. I cannot believe I still remember all those acronyms! Then we later discovered that they stopped doing the portfolio. ACE 7 and after you don't know how lucky you are!

Despite the overwhelming workload, we somehow managed to make the most of our ACE experience. Some of my fondest memories are playing ultimate frisbee and stick ball on South Quad, weekend excursions to Warren Dunes, running around the lakes, going to Chicago for a Cubs game, dancing at Coaches, and just walking around campus at night and seeing the Golden Dome. I met so many amazing people throughout my ACE experience, and I stay in touch with a few of my housemates and ACE 5 classmates. In fact, last summer I visited Katie Pytlak, ACE 6, in Boston and met her husband and new baby. She and I lived together in Charlotte and taught at the same high school for one year. I'm sure a lot of you can relate to this scenario: When our students found out we lived together, their adolescent minds jumped to the conclusion that we were dating and there were always remarks about "Mr. Reis and Ms. Pytlak," which Katie and I could only laugh about.

Charlotte was not the mission ACE site where the schools are impoverished and lacking resources. But for me, it worked out because I had tremendous support at my high school and became a much better math teacher for it. Being a first-year teacher is difficult no matter where you are, and due to the support I had from my mentor teacher, my community, and the ACE staff, I survived those first years, stayed at my school for a third year, and realized that I wanted to remain in the teaching profession. When I moved back to my hometown of Portland, Oregon, I chose to work at a school that was more of a typical ACE site. I helped start up a new school called De La Salle North Catholic, which is part of the Cristo Rey Network and serves inner-city, lower-income students. I have been there for seven years now and even though it is more challenging than anything else I have ever done in my life, it spiritually fills me up and gives me a reason to get out of bed in the morning.

I view my job at De La Salle as a vocation and find fulfillment in answering the call to continue to work in Catholic education. If it were not for my experience in the ACE program, I would not be where I am today and cannot imagine finding as much job satisfaction in another career. For me, the rewards of teaching outweigh any of the bad days, annoying students, and weekends spent grading or lesson planning. Teaching is my life and my life is richer because of the students who enter my classroom and partake in the dialogue we call education. ✪

My Shield, My Spear, and My Armor

Araceli Ramirez ✹ ACE 7 Austin

In the midst of my deepest emptiness and sorrow, I encountered God's grace in the strangest of places—in three enduring housemates in Austin, Texas. I was in my second year of teaching and several factors conspired to drive my stress load beyond what I could bear. I had asked for and gained greater responsibility at school. I had begun training for the Los Angeles marathon. I had become my family's therapist, with my mom, my sisters and my nieces calling me regularly to vent about their concerns and life stresses. At the time, my sister was going through a divorce and my nieces were suffering tremendously. All I could think about was, "Here I am in Austin instilling hope, peace, and love in the lives of other families and their children while my own family is in despair." The superhuman person that I once was no longer remained. I felt so helpless. Despite everything and everyone around me, I felt empty. I was overwhelmed with life and too proud to ask for help. I had encountered my greatest weakness—myself.

During happier times, I looked forward to returning home to my Austin community after a long day of teaching and coaching. I would wait in great anticipation to hear Nick gently strumming his guitar, Jill filling the house with warm scents of mom's "gravy," and Michael grinning with gentle eyes and comforting embraces. However, during the moments when I encountered my greatest tribulations, I made every attempt to tune out Nick's sweet music, ignore Jill's gravy, and avoid Michael's gaze. I didn't know what was happening to me or why. I realized the harder I tried to be present to my ACE Austin family, my students and the school community, the more distant I became. It seemed the more I needed them, the more I pushed them away. Pushing people away was what had kept me safe and strong for so many years. I pushed people away before they could leave me, before they could hurt me.

Despite my unbearable ways and attempts to push my housemates away, Michael, Nick, and Jill wouldn't leave. They stuck! It was clear to them that I was suffering and that something had to change. On the day they lovingly, yet firmly, confronted me about their concerns, our encounter was not beautiful or romantic. I quickly defended myself and tried the best weapon I knew of to put distance between us—anger. Yet, in the midst of my rage and cursing, something moved me to stop. I glanced into Michael's eyes and I saw so much pain, yet so much love, that I suddenly felt as if I was looking into God's eyes. I then looked at Nick and Jill and received the same loving eyes. Something inside of me felt warmth and safety. My heart immediately softened and my words of anger soon became tears of sorrow. I abandoned my pride and my anger and embraced their presence.

That moment was the turning point for me. Just as I had sunk into my greatest isolation and pain, God illuminated His grace to me through my three housemates. At a time when I felt desperately alone in the world, God showed me that He had not abandoned me after all. In fact, on that miraculous day, he sent three of his angels to guide me out of the darkness. From that day, I found the strength to seek spiritual refuge, confront my demons, and restore the broken parts of my life.

I have yet to encounter anyone else who has been my shield, Nick, my spear, Jill, and my armor, Michael. They loved me unconditionally and blessed me with a moment that has forever left imprints of God's grace upon my life. ✪

Mathematics of Friendship

Elizabeth Stowe  ACE 12 Biloxi

In friendship, sorrows are divided and joys are multiplied.

I came to recognize the truth in this statement through my ACE experience, which began in Biloxi, Mississippi, in August 2005. I knew ACE would be a challenge, but I never dreamed of witnessing all that I saw.

Hurricane Katrina ravaged her way through our schools and greater community after our third week of classes. She left nothing in her wake. Our building was closed and we combined with another Catholic school down the road. We were out of class for seven weeks, cleaning up the grounds.

The secretary at our new school was Miss Patty Fox. Miss Patty is a woman of great strength. She was the rock upon which her family, her friends, and the school community stood during this time of great trial. She was a beacon of faith and a harbor of hope.

That January, I was able to organize 100 students from Boston College to come down and help rebuild the Gulf Coast. They helped at the ACE schools in the area and worked in the homes of the students and teachers of the schools. The students were able to bulldoze Miss Patty's house, setting her three months ahead of schedule for rebuilding. They walked brick-by-brick, 2x4-by-2x4, to the dumpster on the street. This was a powerful image.

As I stood at Miss Patty's side, she remained the rock she had been for the community. I, on the other hand, was a mess. Tears streamed down my face. It was heartbreaking to witness a home, as damaged as it was, being clawed by a bulldozer, tearing down all that was left from the house it once was. Miss Patty stood strong with a half-smile on her face saying, "This is the first step to rebuilding." That day I was blessed to cry those tears for Miss Patty.

In friendship, sorrows are divided and joys are multiplied.

***

Two years later, after I graduated from ACE, I was able to go back to Pascagoula and visit. Although there is still work to be done, there has been great progress. I stayed in Miss Patty's house during my visit. When I walked in the door, I was overcome with emotion. She was home. She had a roof over her head. She had walls to protect her. She had furniture she could relax in. She had her family, which made it a home. That day I was blessed to cry tears of joy for Miss Patty.

In friendship, sorrows are divided and joys are multiplied.

***

I was blessed to develop true friendships with the people of Pascagoula, Mississippi. They are a people of great faith, great hope, and great love. They inspire me every single day. Through my ACE experience, I learned the mathematics of friendship to be a blessing where sorrows divide and joys multiply.

Why Don't They Come Live With Us?

Jen (Mullins) Podichetty ⊛ ACE 5 Corpus Christi

I spent my two years in ACE teaching kindergarten at Saint Anthony's Elementary in Robstown, Texas. Robstown is a Mexican-American community two hours north of the border, which is infamous to most Texans for its challenging environment and extreme poverty. The school was tremendously under-resourced and was staffed primarily by volunteers. My community member Gary and I tried not to feel overwhelmed after we realized our orientation would consist of, "Here are your keys. If you have any questions, just ask."

From within this often chaotic environment, small miracles happened each day. My first class was one that I will never forget, and one child in that class changed my life forever. Ariana was a living miracle who inspired and challenged me daily. She had suffered a brain trauma at eighteen months, which had affected the functioning of the right side of her body. While in the hospital for the brain trauma, she contracted an infection, which resulted in the amputation of her left leg from just below the knee. All of this would slow most kids down, but not Ariana. She hopped on one leg and jumped rope on two knees. She got her first prosthetic leg just before beginning kindergarten. She was finally more mobile than ever! Yet, because of a difficult family situation, she was angry and had every reason to be. She would hit me, run away from the classroom, and even whack people with her "hard" leg! Fortunately, Ariana quickly progressed through this stage and became the determined person she is today.

Over time, I learned more about Ariana's story. She was the youngest of five children, all of whom had been abandoned by their mother the year before I arrived at Saint Anthony's. Lupe, their great-aunt, had received a call from San Diego late one night. Her niece, the children's mother, had not been back to pick them up in over a week. Lupe caught the next Greyhound bus out to California to pick them up. She returned a week later as a sixty-year-old mother to five children ages four to ten: Ariana, Diana, Salvador, Laura, and Angelica.

During my two years at Saint Anthony's, Lupe and the kids became an integral part of Team Corpus' community life. The five of us ACE teachers—Matt, Molly, Gary, Gina, and I—lived very much like a family. Our strong sense of community was what kept us all going. Lupe and the kids became part of that family. Yet, I could never have dreamed that, after all the tearful good-byes we said that final summer, I would be seeing them all again so soon.

The night before ACE V graduation, Team Falfurrius, made up of the combined Corpus Christi and Mission communities, and our parents ate dinner together to celebrate our time in ACE. During that dinner our collective sadness and worry at leaving Lupe and the kids to fend for themselves in Robstown came up in conversation. Suddenly, my dad asked, "Why don't they come live with us?"

Excitement and apprehension overwhelmed me at the thought of what my dad was suggesting. Would they come? Would Lupe see this as an opportunity or as an insult? How could I ask her without making it seem like we were "rescuing" them? I let the idea go and enjoyed graduation weekend. After all, maybe my dad wasn't even serious. I mean, my parents were almost finished raising their kids. Did they want to start over with five small children, including one with special needs, and their guardian? Yet, on the plane ride home, I knew that my parents were serious about their offer.

When my parents and I returned home to Oregon, I called Lupe. After all my nervousness, her response to the offer was, "Miss Jen, this is what I have been praying for. I just have my five little anchors, so it is hard." With that, everything was decided. Ariana and her older sister, Angelica, would fly out, as a long road trip would be too much for Ariana (not to mention those around her), and the others would drive out in their van filled with what little they had.

They arrived in early September. Our whole town thought my parents were crazy for inviting complete strangers to live with them, but my parents felt strongly that this was what they were called to do. We quickly settled them in my parents' house, the kids were enrolled in the local Catholic school, and Lupe began work as the Hispanic minister for the area. They lived with my family for a year, and then found a place of their own.

That was seven years ago, and the five kids who were so little during my time in ACE are growing up so quickly. Angelica is married, works at a local bank, and has a beautiful baby girl. Laura is a sophomore in college, and Salvador, Diana, and Ariana are all in high school. They all have opportunities that might never have been possible had they stayed in Robstown, but the gratitude goes both ways in our relationship. I am so grateful for Lupe and the kids. They have taught me so much about being thankful, sharing freely, and understanding what it means to truly be a family.

Looking back on the whole experience, it does seem a little crazy, but it also makes all the sense in the world. A group of people had a need, and my family was able to help them. That is what ACE taught me: Do what you can. That is all any of us are called to do. That is what Lupe did when she dropped everything to go and get the kids, and that is what my parents so beautifully modeled for me when they opened their home up to this family.

When I started ACE, I knew I would have an amazing experience, but I never could have imagined how much would come from my two years in Texas. I arrived in Robstown with the hopes of making a difference, and left with a family.

The "Pillar" of Community

Beth A. Burau 🌐 ACE 7 Dallas

"What's taking Bob so long?" I asked. My frustration forced my hand to take the keys out of the ignition. My passive aggressive nature began to kick in. "So, Rosie is not able to make the retreat?" We had been planning our community retreat to San Antonio for a while now. Now, we had lost a participant and with the ridiculous traffic on I-35, Bob's tardiness would tack on hours of travel time. I didn't even want to drive in the first place! I hate driving at night!

I remembered Leti calling me while I was in Minnesota for my grandfather's funeral, during the last week of February my first year in ACE, to check up on me. In the midst of our conversation she suggested a community retreat for this particular weekend and inquired as to whether or not I would be free. My answer was "yes," and a retreat would be great for me and our Dallas "family." Now, waiting in the hot car with the windows rolled down, waiting on roommates who tested my German characteristic of punctuality, I wasn't so sure.

"There's Bob!" Marjorie pointed to the school's entrance.

I glared, using my teacher face. "Where's your guitar, Bob?"

"I forgot it at the apartments. We can do without." That was Bob. Go with the flow.

Great, I thought. There goes the planned music. "Fine. Get in the car." Did anyone notice I was not in good spirits? Soon, Paul's head was sticking in my passenger window.

"Hey, Beth! Can we stop by the airport? I forgot that I have a voucher to claim by today or I'll lose my free flight." Paul, always kind, was a genius when it came to flying. He could get bumped and compensated for flights, regularly. I think he may have actually only paid for one ticket the entire year. "I have to claim it at DFW. Not Love Field."

What?! I was furious! Love Field was closer and DFW International Airport was in the opposite direction of San Antonio! "Fine." I started the car and couldn't look at him for fear of losing my composure. "I'll follow you guys." Marjorie smiled, trying to get me to smile in return.

Finally, we were on our way—just not in our intended direction. We weaved in and out of Friday afternoon traffic without a care for our lives. Did I mention that I hate driving in Friday afternoon traffic?

As we approached the airport, Marjorie signaled for the earlier exit. Great, now what?! She and Paul turned into The Parking Spot. We were nowhere near the airport. They motioned me to follow.

"What are they doing?" I pulled over and refused to move.

"Just follow them, Beth," Ben reassured me, acting as if this were a normal occurrence for Paul. He smiled, "He's probably trying to save on airport parking."

I went into The Parking Spot and parked my car. I figured Paul would take the bus to the airport and back, and then we could be on our way. The Parking Spot bus pulled up behind our cars. Leti, Ben, and Bob got out of the car.

Bob knocked on the window. "Pop the trunk." I obeyed and grunted in frustration. This was ridiculous! At the rate we were going, we would be in San Antonio at midnight! There goes evening prayer!

Soon, everyone started unloading the car.

"Beth, let's go!" Leti called. "We're going to New York!" She motioned for me to get out of the car and began unloading luggage.

Great! Now, we were lying to the bus driver just to get a ride to the airport. "I'm okay. I'll wait here for you guys to get back."

"No, you're coming with us. Get your luggage!"

I grabbed my bag and purse and left the *Gather* hymnals and coat in the trunk. How long must this ruse go on? I scowled and grudgingly entered the bus, dragging my luggage behind me.

"Leti, this is crazy! Why do we have to bring all of this stuff now?" She could tell I was upset. "We're never going to get to San Antonio."

"We're not going to San Antonio, Beth. We're going to New York," Ben interjected. Now, Ben was lying, too. This retreat was becoming more of a disaster.

"No, Beth. We really are going to New York. I called your friend David and he is meeting us tomorrow." Why would Leti bring up my best friend from high school? She knew he was studying at Juilliard and must have figured it would make the lie seem more real. Why was nobody supporting me in my anger? This was supposed to be a community retreat and lying is not good for the soul.

"Good one." I stared down at my feet.

"Really—he is. We're having our retreat in New York City! Surprise!"

I looked around at my roommates, smiles on their faces, and tears began to well up in my eyes. Soon, tears were streaming down my face! New York? Our retreat? David? Surprise?

Paul, with all of his air travel knowledge, found the cheapest airline tickets known to man. Leti and Ben, always good listeners, knew David lived in New York and would be a face from home to brighten my spirits while in mourning. Rosie, Bob, and Marjorie, with their spiritual gifts, helped create a prayerful experience we would not soon forget.

It was then that I realized I had a family in Dallas, my ACE community. Brothers, sisters, mothers, and fathers, who, to bring a smile to my face in the midst of my dear grandfather's death, planned a surprise retreat. They were a pillar upon which I could lean. They became my support.

We prayed in Central Park. We went to Mass at St. Patrick's. We reflected on our spiritual selves and on our ACE community. We grew as a family. We even sang songs to God without Bob's guitar and the *Gather* hymnals, which were still sitting in the trunk of my car. Carnegie Hall, here we come! The only thing I needed to do was buy a coat, since mine was left behind when I thought we would be going to San Antonio.

I will be forever grateful to Rosie, Marjorie, Bob, Paul, Ben, and Leti for this memorable and spiritual experience. I'm sorry for being so angry with you at the time. When is our next retreat?

Oh, Christmas Tree

Thomas Perez ACE 2 Savannah

While living in community is one of the best parts of ACE, it is also the strangest to look back on. Now, more than ten years later, it is almost awkward to tell stories that include the phrase, "one of the women I lived with." I even feel a bit uncomfortable mentioning such a thing to my wife who understands ACE and how at one time this Catholic program encouraged me to live with four women. Still, even with the uneasiness it can cause me today, I cannot think about ACE without remembering a very important lesson I learned about people. This lesson I learned only because I lived in community with five people I hardly knew.

In Savannah, the ACE community originally lived out in the woods on a diocese-owned campground. There were six of us in all, and we were split up so that there were three people each in two small houses. One evening, the three people from my house went to have dinner at the other house. It was nearly Christmas, and when we arrived, there was a small "tree" in the living room of our community members' house. The tree was actually a broken segment from a much larger tree somewhere on the campgrounds. My cohorts had found this large, branchish tree and stood it up in the corner of the room. They had also sprayed fake snow on it to give it more of a holiday feel. My community members looked at us and waited for us to say how wonderful their homemade Christmas tree was. I think I uttered the word, "nice" and then moved towards the kitchen for dinner.

While I did not learn it that night, the three community members that erected the tree were very hurt. Later that year, when we were having community issues, I learned that I should have been more excited about the wonderful tree. I had hurt their feelings by not caring about it. I was informed that I should have cared more because they cared about the tree so much. At the time of this revelation, I could only wonder how I was supposed to be excited about a tree that Charlie Brown would have passed over. The tree had only been a snapped branch sprayed with a cheap can of fake holiday spirit. I didn't get it.

What I have learned since then, though I am not sure when I learned it, is that I didn't need to get it. The simple fact of the matter is that my community members were proud of that tree. They were proud that while living on a very tight budget in a still unfamiliar place, they had made their home a bit special. With a dead piece of wood they had created something that reminded them that it was a special time of year. That stick probably even made them feel closer to their real homes with the real trees that had decorated the Christmases of their youth. I see that now.

I also can see now how important it is to get excited about things that may not really excite you. It is truly a way to show people you care. It is the willingness to share in something that another person finds special. It seems obvious to me today when I attend a student's spring play or watch my students play volleyball. They thank you just for coming out. Without a doubt I have seen the effect when I have spent hours shopping for clothes with my wife or spent time at a function with her family. And not too surprisingly, the excitement comes naturally, and over very little, as I watch my daughters try to write letters or listen to them sing their favorite songs. Anything those two little pieces of me find special is exciting to me.

I am very happy that my time living in community taught me how to share in the excitement of the seemingly banal things that thrill those I care about. I am a much better teacher, husband, and father because of that lesson and because of that Christmas tree. And, when I look back now, I don't really see that pitiful twig I described earlier. I honestly see a beautiful, homemade tree. A tree that was ingeniously fashioned from a gift that God dropped to the ground to help out a group of young teachers that needed a little encouragement during a holiday far from home.

MemphACE Memories

David Archibald  ACE 10 Memphis

As I reflect on being part of the MemphACE community there are so many memories. Some humble me, others bring a deep sense of gratitude, and most others make me laugh out loud. When thinking about our house, I recall a competition between our community and Brownsville to see who could kill more bugs. Though we faired well, Brownsville won by a landslide.

There was also the Memphis in May annual music festival, when several ACE communities came to visit and we were caught in a torrential downpour. Within a couple hours everyone made it back to the house, drenched and exhausted. Although it was uncomfortable walking around in wet clothes and soggy shoes, and the music was cut short, it is still one of my favorite memories of quality time with good friends.

There are many other memorable moments with my MemphACE community, but my time at Memphis Catholic High School was at the heart of my ACE experience. Stories from the classrooms of Memphis Catholic are frequently in my mind today, and I will always cherish those memories of both fun and difficult times.

My first day of teaching taught me that you should never wear a white shirt and tie at the beginning of the year because you might be mistaken for a new student. Thankfully, my mistaken identity and bruised ego didn't last long. Once I established some of Doc Doyle's principles of classroom management, things became much easier.

Detention could be a story in itself, but I distinctly remember one detention involving students reading me their poetry from English class, as well as some boys rapping about my class. Those light-hearted times were deeply appreciated

The Spirit of ACE

and helped me to keep things in perspective.

I have so many memories from my time in MemphACE, but of all the stories I share from my two years in the program, one of the most powerful memories has to do with a note on my desk.

An elementary student from an ACE school in San Antonio was tragically killed in a flood. Steve Holte, ACE 10, wrote to all of the ACE teachers to explain what happened, and to ask for prayers. The end of his e-mail struck me to the core. It read, "No matter what kind of day you are having, make sure your students know you love them."

I wrote Holte's sentence on a piece of paper and taped it to my desk at school. Regardless of what kind of mood I was in or how little energy I had, that note remained a vital reminder of why I was there and of what every ACE teacher is called to do: to be a carrier of God's love. That is what we are about.

At the end of the school year I untaped the note from my desk, but it clearly remains in my heart. Though at a different school, I continue to be challenged to live out its message each day.

My Running Angel

Tiffany Roman ACE 9 Dallas

Without a doubt, Erin Duffy, ACE 10, exemplifies the spirit of ACE. I was blessed with many wonderful roommates in my Dallas community, but Erin did something special that I wish to share with the world. I had the privilege of living with Erin in my second year, which was a blessing in more ways than one. I do not have enough space in this short essay to describe the kindness, patience, and peace that Erin embodies, so you will just have to trust me on this one.

During my first year in ACE, I learned about the annual ACE marathon and decided to train for the half marathon to help me cope with the challenges of teaching a particularly difficult self-contained fifth-grade class. After months of training on my own, I was disheartened when, one week before the race, I found out that I had contracted bronchitis. The doctor informed me that I could not run, so I vowed to tackle the challenge again the following year.

When Erin arrived to the Dallas community in my second year of ACE, I discovered that she ran cross country at Washington University in St. Louis. Erin encouraged me to go for the full marathon and offered to train with me, as she desired to complete her first marathon as well. I wasn't sure I could finish an entire marathon, but I figured, "If Oprah can do it, I can do it!"

Erin turned out to be my own personal Hal Higdon. Not only did she teach me all the techniques that I needed to perform better as a runner, she encouraged me through thick and thin. Our long distance runs bonded us deeply as friends.

As the marathon drew closer, Erin found herself suffering from the constant training and had to stop running due to health reasons. She promised to run the half marathon, but would not be able to complete 26.2 miles at that time in her life. Even though I completely understood, she still apologized profusely as she felt that she was letting me down in some way.

When the day of the race arrived, Erin finished the half marathon before me as she still had the quickness of a university runner. I had decided to run with a pace group on track to finish in four hours and forty-five minutes. It was a smart decision for me personally, as I felt strong when I passed the half marathon mark. Erin spotted me as I trotted by and came out to join me with a gift. As we dashed up a hill, Erin peeled me an orange while running and handed me slices one by one, providing me with an incredible burst of energy. I thanked her immensely for her talents and continued on steadily until mile twenty, when I "hit the wall." I eventually lost my pace group as I simply could not keep up with them anymore. Discouraged, I continued on alone.

I am not sure how it happened, but at the same time I began to falter, Erin noticed me among the crowd. Out of the kindness of her heart, Erin jogged out to where I was in the race and became my running buddy once again. For the next five miles, Erin encouraged me and gave me the mental stamina to keep going. Even though she had already completed a half-marathon, here she was next to me, my running angel.

At the twenty-five-mile marker, Erin quietly slipped off to the side of the road. In shock, I paused and asked her, "Erin, where are you going?" She responded by saying kindly, "Tiffany, this is your race. You need to finish it on your own." Well, at that point, I started to cry, I was so overcome with emotion; a marathon can do that to you! I quickly realized that I could not breathe and cry at the same time, so I had to stop crying. Driven by her words, I charged onwards and crossed the finish line completing the race in four hours and fifty-four minutes.

To this day, I share the story of my marathon as a testament to the kindness of others. Erin proved to me that it is only in giving of ourselves does the journey become worthwhile, a true principle of the spirit of ACE.

The Community of Holy Rosary

Tricia Sevilla
ACE 6 Jacksonville
ACE Leadership 6

My first year of ACE was the hardest year of my life to date, and that includes past experiences with divorce, the death of grandparents, and becoming a principal.

I was assigned to teach middle school language arts at Holy Rosary Catholic School in Jacksonville, Florida, an inner-city school with a 99% demographic of African-American, non-Catholic students. I was naïve but excited—of course I could teach these kids! Of course they'll come to love English and reading as much as I do! I was a Notre Dame graduate and I could do anything!

My soul, my heart, and my mind were challenged to their breaking point. In later years my students told me they purposely planned on ways to make me cry in class, and I did—often. I would come home upset and frustrated that the students didn't like me, that they didn't want to do the work, and that their parents thought I was an inferior teacher. I would wake up feeling physically sick because I couldn't face eleven-year-olds.

That was the year I hit bottom, and the year I learned humility. It was the first time in my life I failed at anything and knew I couldn't control the situation. It was also the time I saw God in everyone around me.

The worst day was November tenth, a Wednesday. When I came home I couldn't stop crying, and I couldn't hide in my room any more. I couldn't do it! I couldn't make myself go to school the next day! My housemates surrounded me, asking me what was wrong, trying to calm me down. I just saw no way out of the fact that, at that moment, I hated teaching and was disgusted with myself for feeling that way. The tears wouldn't stop.

My housemates counseled me to use a personal day. Oh, if only the situation were that easily solved. Some things were against me:

1. Our substitute list was very short.
2. Our substitutes were all being used, including our vice-principal.
3. Our science teacher, Sola Sawyerr, ACE 4, was in the hospital.
4. Our social studies teacher, George Keegan, ACE 2, was also very sick and should be home.
5. I didn't have the courage to tell my principal that I didn't want to go to school—not couldn't, just didn't want to.

Determined, my housemates called my principal and explained the situation. Unfortunately, she only confirmed what I already knew. She knew I was hurting, but she didn't have a substitute for me, and could I try to make it through Thursday and Friday? I wished I didn't have to put her in a situation to ask that, but she was in a bind, and I knew that.

That's when my housemates went into overdrive: Scotty Thomas and Dave Madden were keeping me calm, trying to make me laugh. Julie Maund talked to my principal to see if there was any other solution. Elsje Maassen called her principal to see if she was allowed to use her school's sub-list to find someone for me. And Chris Adrian stepped up to the plate and said he would go to school for me, since they were closed for the holiday.

And that's what happened. My housemates sacrificed their time to help me through my pain. Though Chris and I weren't close, I will never forget that he willingly gave up his day off so I could have one.

Though the year never got much easier, I do know that without my housemates and the faculty and staff of Holy Rosary, I would not be the person or be in the position I am today. I'll never forget how my housemates cared for me. I'll never forget how Sr. Dianne mentored me through that year with her patience and her soothing voice. I'll never forget how Sr. Beverly always had a friendly greeting when she picked me up and drove me to school every day, reassuring me that I was doing a great job with the students. I'll never forget Elsje Maassen who made me get up and told me that I had to go to school, that I wasn't sick and that I had to face the day.

They all gave me strength. They were all community for me. They all were God for me. ☯

Love Letters from Southeast L.A.

Clare Bush  ACE 12 Los Angeles

ACE is a challenging program. While excitement and joy are present during one's two years in ACE, there are many days where one needs the encouragement, support, and love of those around them. One way my community members showed their love was through the writing of notes.

Whether they were slid under my bedroom door, placed on my desk, written on the bathroom mirror, on the fridge, or in my shoe, notes from my community members encouraged me throughout my ACE journey. Many notes occurred on birthdays or holidays, but some of my favorites were on Dr. Moreno's observation days, the anniversary of my Grandma's death, the day I left to chaperone our cheerleaders in Hawaii, and on just some "regular" days. Even some of our visitors got in on the action of writing notes. Below is a taste of just a few of these notes.

February 14, 2006
    Roses are purchased when stoplight red
    Violets not sold unless stoplight blue
    Praise to Clare, Soph, and Bridge
    In this attempt to prove heart warmer than fridge
    Picked up three stems
    To say you're three beautiful gems
        Stella S.E.L.A. Love

February 17, 2006
> Please teach well today, I want you to remain a part of our community. No pressure. We are all counting on you. You'll do fine. If things go wrong, just tell Rachel you know me. I got your back.

February 17, 2006
> Good Luck Today! Break a Molecule!

August 2006
> Good luck this year.
> Matthias needs "good strong women" like you.

October 13, 2006
> My regards on your grandma. I know how special she was to you. No doubt she is proud of her granddaughter.

December 6, 2006
> Happy St. Nicholas Day! There is a treat in your shoe.

May 2007
> Happy Honolulu!

May 28, 2007
> Thanks for sharing your nice clean bed with an 'ole dirty man like myself. We are washing your sheets so the cooties are no longer! Have a great end to your year and I look forward to meeting you sometime.

Though my two years teaching in ACE and living in community have ended, the notes have not. Whether it is a postcard from a housemate's vacation in Europe, a text message of encouragement sent at the exact time I was interviewing for medical school, or an email of sympathy when my childhood dog passed away, my community members still write.

The notes continue; the love continues.

Community is a Texas Marathon

Sarah Bates  ACE 12 Denver

If I would have known in the summer of 2005 that I was about to start a teaching program that not only would require countless hours of energy, prayer, and service, but marathon training as well, I would have turned the other way and quickly handed my application in elsewhere. However, that is where I found myself in the fall of 2006, teaching the sixth-grade class at Guardian Angels in Denver, Colorado, and training for a half-marathon in a city completely covered in ice and snow.

Training for a marathon is not easy for anyone, let alone a graduate student swamped with Master's degree coursework and with a full-time teaching job. So why was I doing it? Besides the obvious physical and spiritual benefits of running a marathon, I started training because my school had been designated as one of two ACE marathon recipient schools for the year. Training for the Cow Town marathon in Fort Worth, Texas, meant even more knowing that crossing the finish line in February would bring thousands of dollars to my school. But what started as a mission to benefit my students became a way for me to find some focus in a life that had recently been turned upside-down by tragedy.

Starting my second year of ACE, I was looking forward to an easy transition. I had already taught the dreaded year of a first-year teacher, and I expected the second year to be much smoother. However, a week into my second year of teaching, I awoke to an early morning phone call from my mother in Ohio, informing me that during the early morning of August twenty-seventh, my uncle had been murdered in his driveway during a random attempted robbery.

There are no words to describe the feelings that one goes through when a loved one has been taken by a violent crime. The feelings of shock, anger, grief, and thoughts of, "This isn't supposed to happen to my family. This is something that you read about in the newspaper or see on TV," constantly played in my mind during that morning and the weeks that followed. The murder was considered a high-profile case in Cincinnati, where it occurred, and I spent most of that day in Denver watching the facts unfold across Internet news sites. To say it was a difficult time for my family and me would be a tremendous understatement. My uncle had left behind three children, a wife, his parents, siblings, and nieces and nephews that all cared about him and loved him very much. I am blessed to come from a close family, and this event was heartbreaking for all of us.

After flying home for the funeral and spending a few days with my family, it was difficult to return to Denver. When tragedy strikes your family, your only instinct is to draw closer. When I did return, it was hard. Things just didn't seem the same. It was hard to find purpose in my daily happenings, life at school seemed tedious, and I felt myself pretending that things were okay, when they often weren't.

A new "purpose" emerged, when marathon training began. As difficult as it was, it gave me weekly goals and structure. It gave me a focus to my energy at school as I planned ways to publicize the marathon and pump up our families and staff around the cause. It also gave purpose to my family in Ohio. My uncle had been training to run the Chicago marathon with his daughter when he was killed. My father decided to come out of marathon retirement after almost thirty years and train for our marathon in memory of his brother. My father's desire to support me and the ACE program, while honoring his brother, meant the world to me.

In addition to giving me personal focus, training for the marathon helped our Denver ACE community feel less isolated within the greater ACE program. Living in a geographically isolated community, it was sometimes hard to see the larger picture of what we were doing without having the Notre Dame connection that all ACE teachers have over the summer. We knew that our Denver community was part of the ACE mission, but after a long day of teaching and running, this mission was often overlooked. It was especially hard to feel this mission during the months of January and February, when our training took place in cold temperatures, on dark evenings, and over ice-covered sidewalks. One thing that kept us going was knowing that close to one hundred other ACE teachers and ACE supporters around the country were training and fundraising as part of the same mission.

This greater sense of mission and community was never more evident than when the day of the race finally arrived. A large group of us flew from Denver to Fort Worth together, including three of my roommates, my principal, four other teachers from my school, and a few parents, all of whom were participating in the marathon events in some way. All were willing to run or walk and support each other in our efforts to raise money for the school we cared so deeply about.

Friends of ACE joined our mission as well, in many cases overcoming their own setbacks and adversities. My boyfriend had been training to run the half-marathon, but due to a ski accident, he had to run the 5-K instead—with a broken clavicle. My close college friend ran the full marathon to raise funds for Catholic schools even though she was not a part of the ACE Program.

In the midst of tragedy, my family found meaning and solace through our participation in the marathon. After traveling from Toledo, Ohio, my 57-year-old father ran the full marathon while my sister ran the 5-K, all to the cheers and support of my mom who made the trip down as well.

It is hard to describe the power that existed when the ACE teachers and all our friends and families gathered that weekend in Fort Worth. The sense of purpose, drive, faith, and love was completely overwhelming. The excitement and jitters we felt when we gathered in prayer that morning before the race gave way to a sense of accomplishment that followed as each person crossed the finish line. I felt so privileged to know I was part of such a brilliant and caring group of people.

When I crossed the finish line that day, and waited with my sister to help my father run in the last mile of his twenty-six, I realized how lucky I was to have such amazing people in my life. To have a family that supported me, a dedicated group of coworkers, close friends, and a loving boyfriend who all ran in support of my ACE school, I realized that ACE is truly a community that one will not find anywhere else. And, as I watched my father push his body to the limits in honor and memory of his brother, I felt nothing but the utmost love and respect for him. As I looked at the various faces of the ACE community that weekend, I knew that my application was definitely handed in at the right place.

I Had Every Reason to Stay Home

Tony Hollowell ✪ ACE 11 Biloxi

I had spent the past year teaching at Resurrection Catholic School in Pascagoula, Mississippi, but after Hurricane Katrina ravaged both the school and the town, I had a lot of good reasons to stay home in Indianapolis. I knew I was going to be out of school for several weeks, I didn't think there was really anything I could do to help, and I thought it would be better to stay home. However, I just felt like I had to go back. I was frustrated with watching the news on TV about all the destruction, and so I loaded up my 1994 Chevy Cavalier with twenty pounds of turkey and ham, eighty hamburger buns, countless grapes and chips, ten gallons of water, ten gallons of gas, and a pair of work boots and gloves and headed back to the town of Pascagoula. The gloves and the boots were the only things remaining after two days.

After spending a few days connecting with my students and surveying the destruction of their homes, I finally made it to the school. I had to sneak into my classroom through a broken window. The first thing I noticed was that my binders for my classes from the last year were covered in mud and sewage, and were essentially ruined. The pain of that thought was eased by the realization that I wouldn't need lesson plans anytime soon! The water line on the wall indicated that the school had taken in approximately three to four feet. With only two classrooms and the library located upstairs, this pretty much ruined the whole school. The water, however, was not the only culprit, because when the building flooded, the toilets overflowed, causing a thick layer of sludge to cover every inch of the building that had been touched by water.

While I had not had a class during my ACE summer that taught me how to clean up a school after a hurricane, the job that needed to be done was very simple. Everything in the school, except for the studs, needed to be thrown away. The only problem was that emptying an entire school can be a pretty daunting task. With everyone working on their own houses, I turned to the man who, next to Batman, can get more things done in one day than any other human: my Dad. I told him about the situation and that we needed generators, shop vacs, pressure washers, gloves, masks, brooms, squeegees, and a whole lot of hands. I told him I would take care of getting the hands if he could take care of everything else.

Within twenty-four hours, my Dad was on his way to Pascagoula with a van full of equipment and supplies purchased with funds donated by people who had heard that he was coming down. On my end, I begged anybody who would listen if they could spend at least a few hours at the school to help get the place clean. I wasn't sure how many people would come, but I was hoping we would have about ten or twenty people there to help out.

The next morning, by eight o'clock, there were at least fifty students and parents at the school ready to go. It was really amazing to think so many people would give so generously of their time to help our school out. Most notable among the crowd were several of my students who frequented my Saturday detention group which I affectionately dubbed the "Breakfast Club." They were some of the hardest workers in the whole group. Maybe they were excited to be throwing away so much of the school!

Anyone who has been a part of ACE knows that, as an ACE teacher, you will be involved in situations that you never anticipated when you signed up for the program, and this was no exception. Here I was, a 23-year-old teacher pursuing his license in science education and a Master's degree from Notre Dame who now was somehow in the middle of helping repair a school after a hurricane. I had no idea why or how this had come to be, but for the next four weeks, I had the same basic routine: I would wake up, go to the school, begin where we left off from the day before, work a full day, and crash into bed. Every day, we had a mob of students and parents ready to clean the school and get it where it needed to be. On occasion, we were blessed by groups of angels who appeared unexpectedly to help us along the way.

One group arrived about a week after the storm at around four o'clock in the afternoon, just as the day was winding down. I looked down the hall and saw five very large silhouettes looming in the doorway. They walked down the hallway, and promptly introduced themselves as firefighters from Oregon who had come down to help any way they could. They were awesome! Our kitchen and cafeteria had still not been touched. They helped move out massive refrigerators, stoves and other appliances and they were a huge help for some technical electrical work that needed to be done. They spent two days at the school, and then we never heard from them again. They were true angels.

Another group arrived just as I was getting ready to spend the day watching the Notre Dame versus Michigan football game—the Charlie Weis debut. No matter. I had been walking around school early that morning, making a list of the many things that still needed to be done. The number of students turning out to help had begun to dwindle, and I was wondering how we would finish all that needed to be done. Unexpectedly, a massive military "assault vehicle" pulled up to our school. Out of the back of this vehicle came fifteen men with three highly valuable commodities: sledge hammers, crowbars, and really, really big muscles. Two men introduced themselves as Captain Yobes and Captain Awad from the Navy Seabees, the Navy's construction battalion. They said they heard our school needed help, and asked what needed to be done. Within eight hours, they had completed nearly everything on the list that I had made in the morning—a list that I thought would not be finished for weeks. They were humble, hard-working people who never complained. They simply asked what needed to be done and did it. They were true angels. On a side note, we hooked up a TV to a generator during lunch and watched the Irish whip up on the Wolverines. It was the best lunch I have ever had.

My Dad only stayed for a few days. He decided to go back home to Indianapolis and tell people about what he saw. By the time he was finished, he had received nearly $50,000 in donations for our school from some local parishes and Catholic schools. Considering our school's entire annual operational budget was $1.1 million, this was a huge sum of money. Once again, our school was blessed by a group of angels.

There were many times during the course of cleaning the school and dealing with contractors and insurance adjusters when I kind of laughed to myself thinking, "What am I doing here? I am a science teacher, not a general contractor!" But my experience was not that different from those of other ACE teachers. Although the aftermath of Katrina was an extreme example, ACE teachers often face demanding situations where there is no right answer or definite plan of action. There are just some tasks that need to be done, and you know you are the person who needs to do them. Christ tells us, "When you have done all you have been commanded, say, 'We are unprofitable servants; we have done what we were obliged to do'" (Luke 17:10).

As ACE teachers, we are not heroes. We are servants. We are people who simply do what is asked of us. And it is our hope that, by doing the tasks that are asked of us, we will begin to rebuild our Catholic schools, our communities, and eventually our world. Each of us has a small gift to offer, but when we put our gifts together, something special happens. My story about the hurricane is really the same story that is being lived every day in every ACE teacher, a simple story of doing what is asked of you, and something good happening from it. In the end, regardless of the outcome, we know that we have only done what we were obliged to do. Anything else is from God's grace.

SPIRITUALITY

"Jesus turned and saw them following him and said to them, 'What are you looking for?' They said to him, 'Rabbi' (which translated means Teacher), 'where are you staying?' He said to them, 'Come, and you will see.'" (John 1:38-39)

"Do not conform yourselves to this age but be transformed by the renewal of your mind, that you may discern what is the will of God, what is good and pleasing and perfect." (Romans 12:2)

Tears to Joy: Daring to Race with the Winds of the Spirit

Lou DelFra, C.S.C.
Director of Pastoral Life
Alliance for Catholic Education

Fr. DelFra joined the ACE program as Associate Director during the program's first year and has served tirelessly in various capacities ever since. Having discovered his vocation to the priesthood through the faith community of the early ACE classes, he was ordained a Holy Cross priest in 2004. After two years at Holy Redeemer Parish and School in Portland, Oregon, DelFra returned to ACE and currently serves as Director of Pastoral Life of ACE and ACE Fellowship as part of his responsibilities with the Pastoral Team and Notre Dame's Campus Ministry. Prior to ACE, DelFra served as a Catholic high school and middle school teacher at Malvern Preparatory School in the Archdiocese of Philadelphia.

"And they left everything and followed him." (Luke 5:11)

Something about the Synoptic Gospels' version of the call of the first disciples has always bugged me. Jesus walks along the Sea of Galilee, sees Simon and Andrew, and later James and John, mending their nets in their fishing boats. He calls out, rather concisely and with no attempt at selling the invitation with job descriptions, perks, opportunities for advancement, or anything else, "Follow me!" And all four disciples drop everything, leave nets and boats and family, and begin to follow Jesus. I only wish I could say this is how it worked out in my own life of discipleship. The eagerness, trust, and immediacy of their response are embarrassingly incongruent with my own response to God's call. Still, there is something resonant about these Synoptic accounts of the call of the first disciples—the explosiveness, the charisma of Jesus, the disciples' attraction to him, the eruption and the disruption in their lives.

Are young people "called" to ACE? Certainly, the evidence is conclusive that they are attracted to ACE, and all it offers—the challenging service, the dynamic outlet for all the classroom knowledge they have just accumulated in college, the fully-funded Master's in Education, the adventure of an assignment in an unfamiliar city in need of their energy and gifts in the context of an abundantly gifted and enthusiastic community of peers. There is plenty to attract them. But are they called? That is to say, called by God? Directed by the Holy Spirit to give these two years—and maybe more—of their lives to ACE and Catholic schools? And to set out on a journey—maybe even a vocation?—that will change the rest of their lives? In brief, is ACE an instrument, used by the Holy Spirit, to help young people discover their vocation?

For those of us blessed to be a part of ACE, the evidence is abundant, compelling, and best understood in the context of the real lives of ACE teachers.

In my third year as ACE's Associate Director, the ACE staff was conducting its entrance interviews for applicants who had been accepted into ACE and then had to tell ACE if they would accept our offer. It was the end of the third and final day of these interviews. A little bleary-eyed, I shook myself fresh to interview one final accepted applicant, Ted Lefere. Fortunately, given my depleted energy, the interview was uncomplicated. Ted was thrilled with his assignment to teach high school religion in Biloxi, Mississippi. "Sign me up!" He walked out, and I breathed a sigh of relief that ACE 4 was finally in place.

I had the good fortune in those days of parking my car in the lot adjacent to Notre Dame's beloved Grotto, a hidden, tranquil, and sacred place of candlelit prayer in the middle of Notre Dame's campus. On my way to the car each evening, I often paused to kneel at the Grotto and say a prayer to end my workday. As I knelt on this day, my eyes were closed in prayer, when I heard the person next to me quietly crying. Not wanting to stare, I only half-turned my head and whispered to this person, "You okay?"

"Never better. I just got into ACE. Guess it's not that exciting to you!"

It was Ted, and his were tears of joy. Moved by his emotion, I asked him if we could pray together. I listened, frankly awestruck, as Ted prayed from deep within his heart in thanksgiving that God had answered his prayer to give him a direction in his life upon graduation that would allow him to share his gifts and his faith with others. As I drove home that evening, I felt this heightened—even oddly unsettling—sense that maybe there was something to those Gospel accounts of being called to discipleship. Maybe ACE was being used by the Holy Spirit to call people to discipleship in the same way. Two years later, Ted returned to Notre Dame as the leader of a retreat for a group of seniors from his high school in Mississippi. We gathered for night prayer at the Grotto, and as I watched Ted lead these students in prayer, I couldn't help remembering the day we knelt there together, and how this spiritual movement within Ted had come full-circle, now shared with a new generation of students.

I remember, too, Jenny Robinson walking into her entrance interview. Her face was full of emotion and tension, and I could tell this would be a charged conversation. What was going on? Like Ted, she was thrilled to have been accepted into ACE, and felt deeply called to be a teacher. But she was in an important relationship, one that she thought was leading towards engagement, and after many weeks of difficult discernment, she concluded that the relationship was calling for her presence. This was a major loss for ACE, as Jenny had received one of the highest scorings of all our applicants that year. I sensed that we both left the room disappointed.

A couple weeks later, ACE 3 was assembled, and all the applicants had confirmed their placements. This settled state lasted all of two days, as in April, one of our teachers in Charlotte, North Carolina, decided to back out. It put us all in a bind—ACE, the Charlotte ACE community, and the school that was counting on ACE for a middle school English teacher. I returned to my office to call Charlotte with the bad news. We were a new program then, and the late withdrawal would naturally lead to suspicions in the diocese about how helpful our program would be.

Early the next morning, Jenny called the office. She was upset and asked if she could talk. When she arrived, she sat down, and told me that she had made the worst decision in her life and would we accept her application again next year? I told her absolutely not—because we needed her this year. I called the superintendent of Charlotte, and Jenny was an ACE teacher. As Jenny told me later, "I cried most of the way to your office and most of the way home—on the way to the office with apprehension, and on the way home with sheer amazement and joy at this gift of grace." Jenny is now also a wife and a mom; she met her husband, Kevin, an ACE teacher in Mobile, Alabama. Their three children—

Katie, Maggie, and Patrick—as well as the children of St. Anthony's School in South Bend, where Jenny continued to teach, have all been blessed abundantly by their mother's change of heart. A good story, yes, but also part of the mounting evidence that the Holy Spirit leads people to their calling through ACE.

Hundreds of ACErs could tell similar stories, but the Holy Spirit's reach doesn't end with them. In 1996, we accepted into ACE an extremely talented and intellectually gifted Notre Dame graduate named Rick Munzinger. Amazingly, Rick felt called to spend two years of his life teaching second grade. Even among the outstanding talent and generous hearts that ACE has attracted, this combination was unusual. There was only one problem: Rick had LSAT scores off the charts, an acceptance to Stanford Law School, a dad who was an extremely successful attorney in Texas, and expectations—from himself and others—of following in his dad's footsteps. Despite all of this, Rick had made his decision to become a second-grade ACE teacher, but, not surprisingly, he dreaded telling his dad.

Finally calling his dad, Rick launched into his well-rehearsed pitch. "I know I've been working towards law school. But I really want to try out becoming a Catholic school teacher. And I want to teach second grade. It's their first communion year," the budding lawyer threw in for good measure to his faith-filled father. There was a moment of silence, and then, says Rick, simply the sound through the phone of his dad weeping and telling Rick how proud he was of him. Rick became an outstanding second-grade teacher, a Stanford law school graduate, and is now a practicing lawyer who does *pro bono* advocacy for families and for Catholic schools.

As you can tell from these few stories—which really do represent just the tip of the iceberg—it has been the privilege of a lifetime to journey with these disciples as they discover the radical life of love and service to which God is calling them, as he called Simon and Andrew, James and John. More than anything, it is awesome to see the lives of joy that result from following the promptings and invitations of the Spirit, even when the surprising force of the call leads in unexpected and initially troubling ways.

As for me, as part of the ACE Staff, each September I traveled to visit the ACE teachers in their classrooms and in their communities. I spent time in conversations with each teacher afterwards—talking about teaching, talking about community life, but most importantly, talking about how they discerned God at work in their lives and where God was leading. In their community, we shared meals together, we prayed together, we shared our souls and wrestled with God together.

In September 1998, as I flew home from Macon, Georgia, and two weeks of traveling from one ACE site to another, I slumped back in my seat, took out pen and paper, and started writing follow-up notes about each teacher and each community. As I revisited each face, each classroom, each person's story as it was unfolding in all its joys and sorrows; as I remembered each night of prayer and faith-sharing, I became overwhelmed by the power of the Spirit at work in our lives. I saw, all at once as in a snapshot, how the Spirit was transforming so many lives, inviting each one of us to a deeper, more challenging, and more joyful life—all through the service of others. When I got home that night, I threw my bags on my bed, and inexplicably, I just started to cry. I had felt for some time that God had been calling me to give my life as a priest, but the sacrifices had seemed too much, the way of life too uncertain and unexpected, the risk too great. I cried, then cried some more, wrestling and watching as my objections evaporated in the wake of the witness of the past two weeks. I cried so hard that I finally passed out! I woke the next morning, still lying atop my bed, next to my still-unpacked suitcase, and—inexplicably—I was at peace. I knew what I wanted. I knew what God was calling me to do. And I felt the overwhelming compulsion and peace of realizing that those two were the same thing. I was ordained a Holy Cross priest on April 17, 2004, and today gratefully serve as chaplain to the ACE teachers and the ACE Fellowship. I don't move as quickly as Simon and Andrew, James and John, but perhaps, I—and many, many ACE teachers through the years—have heard the call that they heard that day by the sea. And we have discovered the joy of following.

We Cannot Do Everything

John Daily ⬤ ACE 7 Mission

The following selection is taken from a speech given at the Immaculate Conception School (ICS) 2007 Alumni Banquet in Rio Grande City, Texas. John Daily, ACE 7, had the good fortune to teach in the middle school at ICS from 2000-2002.

I was first introduced to the prayer "Prophets of a Future Not Our Own" when I arrived in The Valley because one of the previous ACE teachers in our house in Mission had pasted excerpts of it around our house. I think the prayer beautifully captures the mission of Catholic schools and role that the parents, teachers, administrators, and supportive alumni play in making ICS such a special place. I would like to share it with you tonight:

> It helps now and then to step back and take a long view. The kingdom is not only beyond our efforts, it is even beyond our vision.
>
> We accomplish in our lifetime only a small fraction of the magnificent enterprise that is God's work. Nothing we do is complete, which is another way of saying that the kingdom always lies beyond us.
>
> No statement says all that could be said. No prayer fully expresses our faith. No confession brings perfection. No pastoral visit brings wholeness. No program accomplishes the Church's mission. No set of goals and objectives includes everything.
>
> This is what we are about: We plant the seeds that will one day grow. We water seeds already planted, knowing that they hold future promise. We lay foundations that

will need further development. We provide yeast that produces effects far beyond our capabilities.

We cannot do everything, and there is a sense of liberation in realizing that. This enables us to do something, and to do it well. It may be incomplete but it is a beginning, a step along the way, an opportunity for the Lord's grace to enter and do the rest.

We may never see the end results, but that is the difference between the master builder and the worker. We are workers, not master builders; ministers, not messiahs.

We are prophets of a future not our own.

A prophet, in the most generic sense of the word, is a messenger or a deliverer. The ICS teachers, staff, parents and alumni are ICS's prophets. In turn, our task is to ensure that the opportunity to receive the gift of a Catholic education is delivered to the children of this community. And just like the prophets in the prayer, we are not perfect. The facilities could be nicer, the books and computers could be newer, the lessons could always be better planned and better taught, and the children could always learn more. But we should not be frustrated by our imperfections. As the prayer says, "We cannot do everything, and there is a sense of liberation in realizing that. This enables us to do something, and to do it well."

The question, then, is "What do we do well?" Saint Thomas Aquinas, the greatest scholar in the history of our Church, believed that our purpose in life is to know and love God. He taught us that faith and reason, working together, enable us to know and love God as the angels know and love God. We cannot know God through reason alone and we cannot know God through faith alone, the two must be working together. This is the true gift of a Catholic education—an intellect grounded in both faith and reason. This is the gift that the alumni of ICS have received and this is the gift that we are called to deliver to future generations.

It is through events like tonight's dinner that we are able to fulfill our role as prophet and ensure that a Catholic education is delivered to the children in Rio Grande City. And while tonight's dinner is a step, it is only one of the many steps that we all need to take to ensure a bright future for ICS. The continued growth and development of ICS is our responsibility and it will be our legacy.

My two years at ICS were one of the greatest gifts I have ever received, and your presence here tonight is a testament to the gift that each of you feels ICS has given to you. Whether it is through our prayers, our time or our donations, we must continue to be prophets for ICS. We need to plant seeds that will one day grow. We need to water seeds already planted, knowing that they hold future promise, a promise our forefathers and mothers kept to us and a promise that we must keep to the children of this community. Thank you.

The ACE American Fellowship Tour: A Closer Look

Karl Franz Flasch Hendrickson ✪ ACE 11 Mobile

"I'm not angry. I'm not angry." The barely audible voice was my own. Like an eager student of a self-help guru, I repeated the words over and over again. "I'm not angry. I'm not angry." However, I was no student. I was a teacher—a science teacher—and I was being pushed to my limits.

This day was different from any regular day in the classroom, though. My anger was not caused by gum chewing, airplane throwing, bullying, or even cheating. I wasn't supposed to be angry at all. I wasn't even at school! I was on summer break and had decided to spend the "three best reasons to be a teacher" traveling with fellow ACE teachers from Los Angeles to New York—on bicycles—to raise awareness and funds for ACE schools. Just east of Amarillo, Texas, the prevailing winds from the west about which we had read so much while planning gave way to a fierce wind out of the east that had me surprised that Pecos Bill didn't show up with his lasso.

***

The ACE American Fellowship Tour was the brainchild of my good friend Tony Hollowell, ACE 11. Along with another good friend, Tony and I roomed together for the second summer of ACE back at Notre Dame. In the midst of my work studying developmental psychology and methods for teaching science, a curious e-mail popped into my inbox. It was from Tony, and was addressed to our entire ACE cohort. "Since we won't be taking classes next summer, is anybody interested in going cross country with me—on bicycles?" I fired off a quick response, "Tony, you're crazy—but I think I'm in!"

Tony's dream of riding his bicycle across the country soon became so much more than just a bike trip. Along with a fancy new name—The ACE American Fellowship Tour—came ambitious new objectives. The seven other riders and I were now riding to meet and network with other educators and administrators involved in Catholic education, to spread and share the mission of ACE and to raise funds to support three ACE schools.

***

Using all the physics I knew, I struggled to crouch and reduce my surface area to combat the effects of wind resistance. I furtively clicked into successively lower and lower gears—my legs careening in circles while my bicycle inched forward.

We were riding on the Great Road, the Mother Road—Route 66. In the previous two weeks there were times the nostalgia was so thick it appeared to be the only thing sustaining life and the local economy in some small towns. Neon signs for motor lodges still blinked prices that probably hadn't changed for a few decades. The signs were not the only things that hadn't been touched in decades—the pavement hadn't either, and my tailbone was taking a pounding.

***

"I'm not angry. I'm not angry." This time I repeated the words to Chelsea Madison, ACE 11, and Mary O'Leary, ACE 11, with whom I was riding that day. I was not alone in my cycling struggles. The usual banter and stream of conversation between riders during each day's ride had dried up in the face of Hurricane Texas. I was beginning to dread the winds that "come sweeping down the plains" in Oklahoma, where I dreamed of Rodgers and Hammerstein standing by the side of the road saying, "We told you so!"

We had already been pedaling for five hours that day, including a stop at the famous Cadillac Ranch on the western side of Amarillo. We had also admired—but passed—the Big Texan Steakhouse, home of the seventy-two-ounce steak. Though we were on four- to five-thousand-calorie diets, something told me it shouldn't all come from one piece of red meat.

We soon passed a sign that read "Groom, Texas—13 miles." Usually, such a short distance to our day's destination would be a cause for celebration. Today, however, was a different story. A quick check of Chelsea's bike computer revealed a speed somewhere between nine and ten miles per hour. I knew that even my students could do this one: thirteen miles divided by nine miles per hour means almost another hour and a half of riding. "Ow!" cried my tailbone. Morale sank to a new low.

***

Like a new ACE community, the bike trip brought together eight riders from seven different ACE communities. Each night before bedtime we would meet for a team meeting to go over the next day. Coach Tony liked this, because he usually had three or four people he wanted to scold for not "showing enough hustle" that day. Truthfully, it was just like coming home after a day in the classroom. We shared our struggles, we shared our joys, and relived the day's ride. We would then cover the next day's "lesson plan."

We closed each day with a reflection or meditation prepared by one of the riders. For me, this was a favorite time of the day. Each rider brought a different perspective and outlook on the day's challenges and blessings and how God's hand guided us through it all. Often we invited host families to join us in our reflection. Many were glad to do so; one evening in particular our host mother insisted that her teenage daughter and her friends join us. She said, "I want them to see young people who believe that God is important, that faith is important, and who are trying to make a difference in the world."

***

Trying to make a difference in the last thirteen miles of the ride we left Route 66 to ride on the shoulder of Interstate 40. Ever the physicist, there wasn't anything I could do about the wind resistance, but I thought perhaps I could find a smoother road to reduce the friction between my tires and the ground. Much to the dismay of my tailbone, the road was no smoother than the Mother Road. Riding on the rumble strip would have been smoother. The two roads, 66 and I-40, ran along side each other at this point. Route 66 seemed to plead like a routinely scolded child, "I won't be bad this time! Give me one more chance!"

I only lasted a few uncomfortable miles on I-40. Mary thought I had finally lost my mind when I screeched to a stop, which was not hard to do from nine miles per hour in a headwind, clicked out of my pedals, and lifted my bike high above my head and announced to no one in particular, "I'm getting off this blasted highway!" It didn't matter; my words were swallowed by a gust of wind. I turned and marched straight through the ditch back to Route 66. Incredibly, 66 at this point was slightly smoother than I-40—at least in the same sense that 150-grit sandpaper is smoother than 100-grit sandpaper. "Thanks," said my tailbone. I think it was being honest, but I barely heard it above the howl of the wind.

***

"I'm not angry. I'm not angry." Chelsea, Mary, and I pushed on, and I prayed for the endurance to finish the ride. As Groom slowly came nearer, I was greeted by one of the more magnificent man made sights of our whole cross-country trip. At the western edge of this tiny panhandle town stands the second tallest cross in the Western hemisphere. Towering to a height of nineteen stories, and visible for up to twenty miles in each direction, this white steel cross silently but incessantly proclaims the Word of salvation to all who pass along the busy interstate. St. Paul tells us that the cross is the power of God to those who believe. For me, it provided enough inspiration to keep pedaling for the final hour on the road, even as I slipped further and further behind Chelsea and Mary, whose endurance visibly outlasted mine.

Cycling in solitude, I watched as the cross rose higher and higher above the wheat fields around me. I realized more and more that the harder I tried, the more futile my struggle became. Jesus' words to St. Paul flashed through my mind: "My grace is sufficient for you, for power is made perfect in weakness" (2 Corinthians 12:9).

I had to let go. My legs kept going, but I could not fight the wind and the road anymore. The more I let go, the more His peace came over me. The more His peace came over me, the more I realized, "I'm not angry." I finally limped into Groom—broken and battered in body—but still in one piece, and mostly at peace. ✪

My ACE Mission

Laura Cunniff  ACE 12 Mission

As I looked down the two pews of quiet children during our Masses every Friday, a sense of peace, calm, and purpose would fill me. I would follow my fourth-grade students up to receive Communion, and I knew that this is where God was calling me to be. There, at Immaculate Conception School in Rio Grande City, Texas, one mile from the Mexican border, we would offer up classroom prayers on Thursday mornings, and I felt the Lord with us. When the kids recited the Ten Commandments, I hoped that these words would become an important part of their faith lives. Our school prayer in the mornings included "San Isidro Labrador, manda el agua y quita el sol," translated "Saint Isidro Labrador, send the water and take away the sun." My ACE community members and I coached basketball, and would lead our teams in prayer on the bus to away games. That prayer would always end with a Hail Mary, followed by, "Our Lady of Guadalupe, pray for us! Our Lady of Victory, pray for us!" Prayer was everywhere.

When the ACE Mission community gathered for prayer on Wednesday evenings, we would open up to each other on a spiritual level that is so unusual for most people in their early twenties. I would look around our living room as my four other community members talked about their struggles with challenging students or family issues, and realize what a sacred time this was. I was blessed to be a part of a group who not only shared a vocation, a grocery bill of under $100 a week for five people, and a home, but also shared the desire to open up on a deeper level.

The prayerful Mexican-American culture and the spirit found in the ACE Mission community have made me a stronger and more faith-filled Catholic.

Although I have moved back to the Chicago area to be near my family, and pursue my desire to work with a Hispanic community, I often feel that something is missing. I will always cherish the opportunity I had in ACE to openly share my faith and beliefs with others. I am not sure what my life's next mission will be, but my experiences in Mission and Rio Grande City, Texas, have taught me the joy of a life lived through faith. ✪

The Privileged Work of the Holy Spirit

Ted Lefere ✪ ACE 4 Biloxi

I imagine that there are few graduates of the University of Notre Dame or of ACE who are not familiar with the influence and authority of the Reverend Theodore Hesburgh. In light of his multitude of life accomplishments and accolades, his favorite prayer stands as a simple but fervent testimony to a great faith: "Come, Holy Spirit." I have carried those three words close to my heart throughout my life, and they have marked some of my highest and lowest moments. In reflecting upon my ACE experience, I first think back to the spring of 1997. My Notre Dame undergrad days dwindled, and the thought of a life beyond the shadow of Our Lady was at once exhilarating, and daunting. I prayed "Come Holy Spirit." The response was clear. I was drawn to service. My parents, two dedicated "servants" themselves, had instilled a great value for service in my heart, and I was eager to seize the opportunity to live out that value myself.

An article in *The Observer* inspired a phone call to the ACE office. Lou DelFra happened to field my deluge of questions that day, and it was clear that he had unbridled enthusiasm for, and an honorable commitment to, the pillars of ACE. His attitude was echoed in every member of the ACE staff and interview committee. I was intrigued. As a beneficiary of the Catholic schools of Jackson, Michigan, and with a degree from the University of Notre Dame nearly in hand, it seemed to be a unique opportunity: to serve the greater Catholic education community that had nurtured me for so long. Still, the commitment was significant. So I prayed, "Come Holy Spirit." The response was again quite clear.

I humbly accepted a position in ACE 4, and an assignment as a theology teacher at Mercy Cross High School in Biloxi, Mississippi. I began the MAT coursework that summer, and met my talented, dedicated, and colorful classmates and our professors. Their diligence, their intelligence, and their commitment inspired me. The classes soon ended, and the assignment grew near. Again I prayed, "Come, Holy Spirit."

In Biloxi, I found a school and a community lacking many resources, but with an abundance of faith. I dug into the curriculum, I challenged my students, and they challenged me. I wanted to help, and I tried to matter. Measurable progress was elusive. The school year ended, and another summer with my fellow ACE teachers rejuvenated me. Soon, I was back in Mississippi. With renewed confidence, I tackled the curriculum, and the students responded better than before. It was then, somewhere in that second year, that I fully realized the overwhelming privilege of my ACE service.

In ACE, I saw the Holy Spirit at work through an inspiring community of believers, educators, and servants. The people of ACE proved to be a buoy of support in a sea full of challenges. In my classmates, particularly my roommates, I found committed, talented, faithful peers. Their friendships and their support sustained me. In Biloxi, despite many obstacles, I still found a school and a community that opened their arms and their minds, and allowed me to serve. The faith of my students, the diligence of my fellow teachers and our administrators, and the warmth of the families of Mercy Cross High School enlightened me. The opportunity was all made possible by ACE. What an honor.

I believe now that ACE had found me, instead of the other way around. I was a privileged servant, nothing more, but nothing less. And I became a better man because I had completed the many tasks of a servant. But, I still wonder: did my students grow as I did? In my desire to serve, did I educate, and did I inspire? Did I at least get out of the way? More poignantly, when Hurricane Katrina ravaged the Biloxi community in which I served, was the Spirit that had worked through me still at work amidst the suffering? So today, I still pray, "Come Holy Spirit."

The response is as clear today as it was ten years ago. Show me an ACE teacher, and I will show you the work of the Holy Spirit.

An ACE Parable

Keiran Roche  ACE 13 Mobile

Jesus and the ACE Teacher
Based on "The Woman at the Well" (John 4:7-30)

Now an ACE teacher came to the computer to prepare some lessons and Jesus said, "Prepare some lessons for me." The ACE teacher said to him, "How is it that you ask me to prepare more lessons? I have got papers to grade, community dinners to cook, prayers to organize, and teams to coach."

Jesus replied, "If you only knew the Gift of God! If you knew who it is that asks you for some lesson plans, you yourself would have asked me, and I would give you living lesson plans."

The ACE teacher answered, "Sir, you have no Notre Dame Master's Degree and I have six lessons each day to prepare; where are your living lesson plans? Are you greater than Doc Doyle, who gave us the lesson plan template, greater than the ACE support staff, the lectures, and supervisors?"

Jesus said to the ACE teacher, "Whoever writes in this lesson template will have to write another one again; but whoever writes in the template that I shall give will never have to write a lesson plan again; for the lesson plan template I shall give will become in you a lesson reaching up to eternal life."

The ACE teacher said to him, "Give me this lesson template, that I may never have to write another lesson, and never have to sit at a computer again." Jesus said, "Go, call your housemates and come back here." The ACE teacher answered, "I have no housemates." And Jesus replied, "You are right to say: 'I have no housemates'; for you have not chosen to live with the people you do."

The Spirit of ACE

The ACE teacher then said to him, "I see you are sent here by John Staud. You are here to build community in the house."

Jesus said to the ACE teacher, "Believe me, ACE teacher, the hour is coming when you shall worship the Father, but that will not be in the classroom. But the hour is coming and is even now here, when the true worshipers will worship the Father in spirit and truth; for that is the kind of worship the Father wants. God is spirit and those who worship God must worship in spirit and truth."

The ACE teacher left the lesson plan template on the computer and ran to tell the community what had just happened. ⊕

Rejection, Then Acceptance

Eric T. Pernotto ACE 10 Brownsville

August 13, 2003: Prayer written in my journal at the start of my first year of ACE:

Heavenly Father, if it is my purpose to be here, which I honestly believe it is, let me do my job well and teach these students and show them how to be more like you. Keep me motivated, inspired, and focused. You have a plan for me, and though it can be frustrating at times, I am doing what I need to be doing right now. It may be a struggle, but one day, I know that I will be satisfied with all that I tried to accomplish here. Until then, give me patience and wisdom. Bless my school, my students, my community members, and every other person who I have met along the way and who have blessed me with this wonderful life that I live. Amen.

As perhaps many ACErs can confess, Spring Break of my senior year was a difficult week for me. As I focused my time and energy on the mission trip to the island of Tobago I was involved in, the thought that permeated my mind was acceptance. I knew the decision was ultimately in God's hands, but I had bargained and debated with God on why service in ACE was what He needed for me to do. Everything about the ACE program was right. I would have an opportunity to surround myself with strong, faith-filled individuals and share my life with my community members, as well as sharing my knowledge and experience with the youth of Catholic schools. I would be teaching and serving others in God's name. I knew that I was dedicating myself to a higher purpose. I knew that working with youth would be my way of being His hands in the work I deemed to be most important in the world. I felt I knew what I needed more than God did.

This ongoing debate in my heart tore at me, so much so that on one of the final nights of the mission trip, I went off alone into the forest and prayed. We were staying at a Christian camp on the island, and the evening worship service was in full effect. As the minister passionately spoke about faith, my mind was elsewhere. The internal struggle in my mind of fear that I would not be accepted coupled with my firm belief that I was perfect for a position as an ACE teacher was driving a wedge into my relationship with God.

"I leave it to you," I remember praying. "I'm giving up ACE because I know that You know what is best for me." As I spoke these words, I knew exactly what I was doing. A few times before in my life, I had stressed and worried about things I deemed important. These struggles in my life always found me on the losing end of what I felt I needed in my life, though each time, God provided a plan that was even better for me in the long run, whether through a longer wait on my part or a completely alternate plan. This time, though, I simply had not been able to give up my plan for serving in ACE. In my mind, no plan God had for me would be as right as serving in ACE.

The letter came. I was not accepted into ACE.

The waiting list was where I would stay, yet I clung to the possibility that there would be openings as other students sifted through their post-college decisions. I waited. I knew in the back of my mind that ACE was still what God had planned for me. How could God possibly not want me to participate in a spiritual, service-driven program like ACE?

It was a Monday afternoon in May when I received my rejection letter from the ACE office. "Thank you for your interest. We don't foresee any positions for the upcoming year. Best of luck to you in your future plans." My time on the waiting list had expired. There would be no further positions in ACE that would be available for me.

While the dream had been gone for quite some time, the finality of it in print was painful. The dream of teaching in ACE that year was officially dead. I accepted defeat. I was confused, lost, dejected. There was no firm Plan B in my life. I scrambled to look at other options, yet none filled me with the sense of purpose I had seen in serving Catholic school communities. Three days later, I got a phone message from John Schoenig. There was an opening that had just occurred that day at the ACE community in Brownsville, Texas. As I sat on the phone with John late that night, my mind was spinning. Where in the world is

Brownsville, Texas? Facts were being spouted at me, but all I could register was that God's plan and my plan had been the same all along.

Nearly five years have passed since I first started my time in ACE. As I look back on who I was before I entered ACE, I recall possessing an idea about how much of an impact the overall experience would be, but today realize that I didn't, in fact couldn't, really understand the magnitude of what my service would be. Throughout the two years, I struggled with my effectiveness in my community and in my classroom. There were times when I felt I couldn't reach my students or provide opportunities for them to grow. I trusted in God that this was what I was meant to do, and in each of my struggles, He provided a sign to me that I was in the right place.

There was one evening in particular, during the fall quarter, which stands out to me. I was going through the usual stress of being a second-year teacher, overcome with responsibilities, tasks, and expectations. In every sense, I felt as though I was failing as an ACE teacher. My supervisor had recently observed my class, my principal gave me some constructive criticism, and I was simply overwhelmed with all that I expected of myself. That particular fall evening, I was at our school's carnival fundraising event. Again, I had to walk away to talk to God. Lacking a mission trip or a forest, I sat in my car, contemplating driving home and once again asking God, "Is this really where I am supposed to be?"

I composed myself and headed back from my car to the lights and music. Along the way, I saw a seventh grader I had taught named Andrea. She had been my student the year before, and had left to attend public school. I remembered Andrea being a very quiet student. She didn't stand out in any particular way, and I had been pretty confident that I had done nothing to make an impact in her life. Yet, Andrea walked up to me and said, "Mr. Pernotto, I really like the way you taught me last year."

I couldn't believe it. A year and a half before, God's answer to me had been delayed until the last possible moment. This time, his answer came in a matter of minutes. While I would love to say that Andrea, the answer that God sent to me, was enough to increase my efficacy as a teacher for the rest of the year, not surprisingly, in the days to come I did not find a real miraculous transformation or unnatural change. What I did find was a moment of grace, one that I reflected back on when times were low, and one that I have carried with me ever since. Just a brief moment, but an experience that strengthened my resolve to do God's work, and to help me work each day to share that grace with others. God's plans for each of us are always in action, and His answers are there for us exactly when we need them.

I had always been told that God answers prayers, but according to His own timeline, not ours. I will never know what would have happened had I not joined the ACE 10 class, or had I been accepted immediately. I'm sure it would have been in another house, a different community, teaching an entirely different set of students. For my life, there could not have been a more perfect placement, a more wonderful set of housemates, or a more exciting teaching and service experience than working in the Rio Grande Valley. The students and families that I worked with were so influential to me, and I know that in a little way, I made an impact on them as well. God works in mysterious ways, and He certainly taught me to appreciate every single moment of my two years of teaching in the ACE program.

Encountering God in Failure

Tisha (Greenslade) Frost ✪ ACE 8 Baton Rouge

"Now Jesus loved Martha and her sister and Lazarus. So when he heard that he was ill, he remained for two days in the place where he was." (John 11:5-6)

I find it ironic that because Jesus loved Martha, Mary, and Lazarus, he stayed away! This started me thinking about my experience in ACE and my many failures. While I will always be grateful for my invaluable experience and education in ACE, I continually think about my fellow ACErs who are doing incredible things to change the world, but at the end of the teaching day, at the end of the ACE retreat, at the end of ACE graduation, they go home and cry because they feel like a complete failure.

Going through ACE was somewhat like getting the wind knocked out of me. When I finally caught my breath at graduation, I asked, "What just happened to me?" Almost five years have passed since graduation and if somebody would ask me to summarize what I learned in one word it would be failure.

Failure?! We are talking about ACE! ACErs are like the cream of the crop! Not only are ACErs abnormally inspirational (remember watching your first ACE promo video?), not only are they abnormally gifted (remember the older ACErs sharing lesson plans with you and being in awe?), not only are they abnormally funny (can we say talent show?), but they are abnormally talented in athletics, in the arts, and in just hanging out (yes, you can be talented at that).

I had already been somewhat of an overachiever, but it was definitely heightened during ACE. I too wanted to be abnormally inspirational, abnormally gifted, abnormally funny, abnormally talented, abnormally perfect.

The Spirit of ACE

And so it was that, during ACE, I learned to hate failure.

It's not that the thought hadn't occurred to me before. The Beast of Perfection had been rumbling inside for years, just begging to be let out, and it finally saw an open door. I soon found myself feeding it constantly, training it daily, and heeding it without question. It fed off my seemingly innocent desires of success and perfection. I set out to be the best teacher, the best community member, the best mentor, the best lesson planner. I wanted it all!

Wanting it all. That's not a crime, you proclaim! That's not a beast! Wanting it all. Why, that's what drives the world! Indeed, it has since the very beginning. We wanted to "become like the gods" (Genesis 3:5) and have it all. It is in our very human nature, our very fallen human nature that is, that we despise our shortcomings, our limitations, our potential for failure.

But what happens when, inevitably, yes inevitably, we fail—hugely, publicly, totally? We all have our own stories of failure from ACE and even now in our everyday lives. The day—or many days for some of us—when we woke up with no lesson plans ready for our class, the parent phone call gone wrong, the unruly fifth-hour class that just won't behave, the community tension in the house, the list could go on and on.

As ironic as it may be, most of us, when confronted with failure, continue to believe that we are like gods. Yes, of course, we see ourselves as gods in our success and quest for perfection, but also, and more importantly, we continue to see ourselves as gods in our failures. And it is this latter attitude that is far more dangerous.

Because if in our success we believe the world lives, it is in our failures that we believe the world dies. We despair to the point that we believe that because of our failures everyone and everything else has failed, including our God. We are turned so far inward that we see only ourselves, our shame, our humiliation, our defeat. And we can't stand it. We ask: What good am I doing? What have I accomplished? What am I really worth?

"God chose the foolish of the world to shame the wise and God chose the weak of the world to shame the strong" (1 Corinthians 1:27-28).

We cannot be afraid of failure. We must remind ourselves that God himself chooses foolish and weak things of this world. He chooses death, the ultimate failure, according to the world. When he was up on the cross, the world laughed at him. All of his apostles except one had abandoned him. Death was eminent and it seemed that his entire life had been meaningless. But did he not change all of eternity and bring salvation to the whole human race?

We cannot look to humans, trying to become like gods, to show us what failure means. We must look to God, becoming human, to show us what failure means. It is Christ's ultimate "failure," his death, that lies at the very heart of our Christian faith. It is in our failures, when we are utterly humiliated, ashamed, and empty, that we come face-to-face with Him. And He doesn't just put up with us. He runs to us. He embraces us. He carries us.

This is a hard lesson I am still trying to learn four years after ACE. I am much more content with success than failure, but that is not what God has given me over the last few years. Granted, there have been many mini-successes in the classroom, in the parish where I work, with the students I encounter, but overall He keeps letting me fail. And in these failures, I cry out, "If tomorrow I couldn't do anything for you Lord, would you still love me?"

And He reminds me, "In the eyes of the world you might not have done much. But it is your being, not your doing that gives you worth. If tomorrow you couldn't do anything but lie there in bed, I would still love you as much I ever have."

So if tomorrow you wake up and find that all you have worked for and all you have accomplished has been stripped away, remember, Christ changed the world through his "failure." You can still change the world. Have hope in your failure.

Idealist Without Illusions

Michael J. Werner ACE 8 Tucson

Broken glass. The first thing I noticed about the Tohono O'Odham Reservation was broken glass. The second thing I noticed was the abject poverty. The third thing I noticed was isolation. This isolation was not only the isolation I felt pervaded the Tohono O'Odham Reservation, but also the isolation I felt as I first set foot on the "Res." My feelings of isolation, not those of the Reservation, were quickly coupled with strong feelings of helplessness for those living there, and bewilderment beyond any I had felt in the past. These feelings spawned an array of questions, questions that would surface on an almost daily basis for the next two years of my life. Where am I? Where did all this broken glass come from? Am I still in the United States? Is there no floor in that house? How can this be the United States?

The second time, fiftieth time, and even my last time going to the Reservation, these feelings—isolation, helplessness, and bewilderment—still swirled in a fever pitch within me. As my first semester as a teacher at San Xavier Mission School slowly moved along, another feeling began to squeeze out my initial feelings. No longer were feelings of isolation, helplessness, and bewilderment the predominant emotions I felt when driving by run-down, government-provided housing, or the Tohono O'Odham Cemetery, filled with people who died far too young from a disease that is all too manageable—diabetes. No, isolation, helplessness, and bewilderment were not predominant any longer. Frustration took over my feelings of isolation, helplessness, and bewilderment like a tidal wave, leaving these feelings as nothing more than a slight tinge of pain and confusion in both my heart and mind. Frustration was, and still is, the overwhelming emotion I feel when thinking about my time as a teacher at San Xavier Mission School.

This feeling of frustration does not come from the O'Odham themselves. The O'Odham are the most amazing, caring, and culturally-rich group of people I have ever had the opportunity to spend time with and get to know. Frustration comes from the fact that the abject poverty, the isolation, the conditions I witnessed every day on the Reservation are present in the United States. When I think about places where abject poverty runs rampant, areas of the United States do not immediately come to mind. In fact, they never come to mind. Visions of India, Central or South America, and other third-world countries are forefront in my mind. I do not think about any place in the United States. This, however, is wrong. Abject poverty is far too common in the United States, not just on Native American Reservations, but also in our major metropolitan cities, our hometowns, even on our own block. The rewards of working with the O'Odham are many. Perhaps the greatest of these rewards is the frustration of seeing the condition of their native lands and their lives and how this frustration and realization has left me with the motivation to work to better people and their lives.

I take great strength from the O'Odham. No matter how bad things got, or how severely conditions worsened, you could always see a smile, hear a giggle, or see a pair of young eyes filled with hope at school. However, to quote John F. Kennedy, "I am an idealist without illusions" and realize that without help, these eyes filled with hope will slowly cloud over with despair. There are many things I can do to help the people on the Tohono O'Odham Reservation as well as people all over the world. I can donate money, time, and materials, as I have done in the past and will continue to do in the future. I can lobby for change and help awaken the rest of the country to the problems of poverty in the United States.

Some things in this world will go unchanged. This is a fact. People, however, change. This, too, is a fact. I may not be able to change some things in this world, but I can, and will, do my utmost to help people change for the better. Helping people may ease, not cure, but ease, the frustrations I feel when thinking about the conditions I witnessed on the Tohono O'Odham Reservation—conditions I also know are right down the street from our own homes. As I drove off the Reservation for the final time, the glass sparkled and glittered among cacti and various pieces of trash, hurting my eyes and my heart.

Lenten Reconciliation

Kevin Somok  ACE 11 Austin

It was a tough time for Rachel in sixth grade. For years, several of the boys had habitually picked on her on the playground, and it seemed like she had no close friends among the girls. A few in particular were downright vicious to her. Her home life was in shambles, as she was in the middle of an ugly custody case stemming from her parents' recent divorce. Rachel's mother also decided that she did not want her daughter at a Catholic school as the decision was the father's, and refused to send her to school in the standard school uniform. This lack of conformity provided more ammunition for malicious classmates. On more than one occasion, Rachel disclosed to me that she'd thought about killing herself.

With the help of the administration, I took all approaches that I could think of to deal with this issue. We achieved varying degrees of success with individual taunters and harassers, but the fact that Rachel was for all purposes ostracized from the rest of her class didn't change. Her school days continued to be miserable.

All of our Catholic students, which is to say the vast majority, went to Confession during the school day once every Advent and Lent. On this particular occasion during Lent, part of the penance assigned for most of the students by the pastor, Fr. John, included apologizing to and asking forgiveness from those peers or teachers whom they had wronged. This took place at the end of the homily after Fr. John had spoken about our need for forgiveness.

My gut reaction was to consider this a well-intentioned gesture by the pastor, perhaps an appropriate penitential exercise or possibly a pedagogical moment students would reflect upon at some point in the future, but I had doubts as to whether this exercise would bear any immediate tangible fruits in our sixth-grade classroom. And to be sure, I saw some inseparable buddies exchanging goofy and seemingly disingenuous apologies for offenses that may or may not have actually occurred.

In the middle of this, I saw Monica approach Rachel, who sat in the pew just in front of me. Monica was one of three sixth-grade cheerleaders in an otherwise seventh- and eighth-grade dominated squad, and she was the leading candidate for the title of Sixth-Grade Queen Bee. I'm not sure I'd ever before seen Rachel and Monica ever talk to each other. I overheard most of Monica's remarks to Rachel:

"Rachel, I know I've said some really, really mean things to you in the past. I'm sorry. Things are going to be different from now on."

I was glad to hear this sort of conversation. But while I had no doubts as to Monica's sincerity in that moment as we celebrated Mass, I was sure that I knew middle school kids too well to entertain any illusions that this gesture would radically alter sixth-grade social dynamics.

Later that morning, however, I saw Rachel seated with Monica at the lunch table—an Untouchable seated next to the Queen Bee. This continued into the following week. One of the other cheerleaders, who had been even more severe to Rachel than most of the other girls, started to chat with her at recess. Taking their cue from the Queen Bee and a member of her court, several other girls of varying social rank started to include Rachel. No doubt, some had wanted to earlier, but they were worried they risked losing whatever social standing they did have if they associated with Rachel the Untouchable.

I didn't teach this group of students as seventh graders, so I largely lost track of the complexities of their social interactions. Fast forward to eighth grade, when I again had them for two courses. In a fairy tale world, Monica and Rachel would have become BFFs and Monica would have completely given up all those nasty behind-the-scenes tactics that are necessary to establish and maintain the title of Queen Bee. And this is certainly not the conclusion of this story, for Monica was still very much the Queen Bee and she continued to work hard to retain her position. But Rachel was well accepted by the girls, if not by all the boys, and she confided to teachers that she was happy. One scene sticks out in my mind to illustrate the contrast from the first half of sixth grade.

During the eighth-grade retreat day in their final days of school, the kids shared memories and prayer together. They reflected on how much they'd grown in their three, five, or even ten years together. There were giggles and more than a few tears flowed. We then hopped on a city bus to head up to the cathedral to attend the noontime Mass, followed by lunch at Mr. Gaddy's Pizza.

In the restaurant, one table of boys took full advantage of the buffet-style all-you-can-eat arrangements. If memory serves, fourteen slices won the inevitable impromptu eating contest. Then there was the coed table, perhaps a bit more mature in the manner and conversation. They reminisced and spoke of looking forward to high school. Lastly, there was a table of girls fully engaged in girl-talk. And at the center of attention was a beaming Rachel, who was one of the only girls "going out" with one of the eighth-grade boys. Of course, adults ceaselessly take the students to task as to what "going out" means when they don't actually go anywhere together except for school and maybe to the movies with six other friends, but it doesn't do the least to prevent middle schoolers from using the term. The tearful scenes from two years earlier seemed a world away.

A lot happened in those two years between sixth-grade Reconciliation and the end of eighth grade, and I'm not naïve enough to believe that I am privy to all of the complexities of the junior high social world. But I believe that Rachel's road from misery at school to social acceptance and happiness began with that day at Mass with Monica, the Queen Bee, who through her subsequent words and actions let the other girls know that it was okay to treat Rachel with kindness and respect. I'm not sure that would have ever occurred without the healing grace of the Sacrament of Reconciliation.

Silhouettes

Kevin Burke  ACE 9 Phoenix

It's midweek. We're tired and the house is dark in the middle of February at that impossibly long stretch between Christmas and anything that might smell like a day off. Slow days, sluggish weeks; all colored gray with the practiced politeness of not really engaging.

Patience, in our second year in Phoenix, is thin at best. The tension of our varied ideas about community, about spirituality runs like wires through the rooms of the place; we've worn ruts avoiding each other.

But tonight we pray. Together.

Tuck, as we gather in the living room, has a bit of the imp in him. There's a glint in his eye I've not seen in a while and he's laying out butcher paper on the floor, dropping markers at random. We are his fifth graders for the moment.

"Draw. Pick two songs that matter. Shut out your day and listen to them. Find a spot, let the music take you and just draw. We'll talk about it after." And he walks out.

Dramatic. Very intriguing, I think, and I'll ask him about it later. For now I head to the front porch. There's no chill tonight, but I can see my breath as I tape the sheet—backlit and blank but for my shadow—to our picture window.

Nothing, as the music—John Hiatt crying love—snakes through my headphones, strikes me as worth sketching so I begin to outline my shoulders, giving some substance to my shadow. Except I keep moving and new shoulders appear. Any slight shift and a new shadow is cast. So I start anew; another sketch, another me, again, and again, until I have a windowful of phantoms.

I came to teaching to struggle, with and for my students. Not with roommates; not myself. I'm failing somewhere, wrestling with a God I'd never thought to ask for help. So I pray, and mean it for the first time in years, trying desperately to find a way to connect all those silhouettes.

A Rambling Answer to a Short Question

Patrick O'Sullivan ⭐ ACE 2 Charleston

Looking back over the last twelve years, one would find it hard to believe that what started out as a chance to simply give back and to serve others would be transformed into a calling. Arriving home after school one day, I was playing with my daughter, Dani, and saw that I had a message to call Tony DeSapio back. Still in the mindset of "Assistant Principal of Bishop Dunne Catholic School," my first thought was that he had found me a math/science teacher, and I quickly called him back. We talked about ACE and, after catching up, he asked if I would be at Notre Dame for the ACE graduation that summer. Fortunately the timing worked out by one day. Less than twenty-four hours after flying back from a trip to Ireland, my wife, Molly (then expecting our second child), daughter, Dani, and I arrived at campus. Stepping on the campus I was reliving ACE all over again—the family, the community, the energy, and Fr. Scully's familiar smile as he mentioned that our second child was on track to be a member of ACE 36.

During that weekend, Tony asked me a short question, but one that did not have a short answer. While an initial answer quickly came to mind, the full answer wasn't nearly as succinct. And you can ask my wife, my kids, my friends, my family, my housemates from Charleston, my students, my next door neighbor, my—well, let's just say, I have a tendency to ramble.

The question, "What sustains you in Catholic education?" The answer that came to mind: Ricky, Tim, Roberto, Adarely, Jackie, Dee, Jennifer, Angela, Reese, John, Teresa—a stream of names and faces of all the students that I had taught and friends that I had made through teaching, each with a unique impact on my life. I know that we all have stories about our kids and brag as if they were our own. In my mind, this is the best answer I can give; these are the memories of what ACE is all about, as we build those relationships that help us to know God better.

My journey in Catholic education began well before ACE, when my parents came to America from Ireland. They made many sacrifices to make sure that we always had the opportunity for a Catholic education. Still, I never imagined that Catholic education would become my life's calling. Thirty-one years ago I first set foot in a Catholic school, and I still walk the halls today. Some of my greatest memories have taken place in those hallways, whether in South Carolina, Texas, or South Bend, Indiana.

Though my childhood was blessed with a Catholic education, it wasn't until college when I began to see the potential for a vocation. With the end of my senior year in sight, I walked from St. Ed's into Notre Dame's Main Building unsure about what the future held: medical school, New York, D.C.? All that changed with a smile from Fr. Scully and his words, "So, how about Charleston, South Carolina?" Before I knew what had happened I answered "yes"—because let's face it, you can't say "no" to that smile—and found myself at the Grotto. It was there that I knelt down and prayed, with no idea that I would soon be sharing in community with Dirk, Mia, and Aimee and the extended South ACE Loop. My prayer must have been heard, because soon it would be these relationships that would allow me to understand more about God and myself.

Like any ACE teachers, these lessons about God and myself often came when I least expected it. For instance, while teaching at Nativity School on John's Island, off the coast of South Carolina, every week one of my seventh-grade life science students would sit with me for lunch and report on an animal that he had hunted or fished for that weekend. On the Monday before parent-teacher conferences, he brought in dolphin to eat. I was stunned. I explained that where I was from, it was illegal to fish for dolphin. He laughed, and explained "not the porpoise, the dolphin fish," known widely as the mahi mahi. He grinned devilishly at me and said, "I thought that you were a biology major." I apologized and asked him not to say anything to anyone. He smiled and said, "Don't worry. My parents never come to the conferences."

But who were the first parents knocking on my door for a parent-teacher conference later that week? Tim's, of course. With a strangely familiar grin on their faces, their first words were: "So, dolphin." With the ice of my very first conference broken, I've never had anxiety about conferences since. Tim went on to be Angler of the Year, run his own business, and we still touch base a few times a year.

There was the time that I gave a lesson on Jesus as Teacher, and to demonstrate "teacher" we watched a clip from *Dead Poet's Society*. Have you ever wondered if your students "got" your lesson? I got my answer a little later in the year when my desk was surrounded with kids, multiple students were talking, and a general chaos reigned. John had been trying to ask a question; I guess I couldn't hear. All of a sudden, there he was, on top of his desk and exclaiming, "O captain, my captain." Everyone went silent. As I stood there, everything seemed to be frozen in time, and at that moment I could have walked away and my teaching career would have all been worth it.

I keep a number of mementos of those first days of teaching. I still keep a VHS copy of *Dead Poet's Society* and the VCR from our house in Charleston to watch it on. For my students' final theology project of the year, entitled "Who Am I?" they were instructed to make a mix-tape that shared a piece of "who they were" at that stage of their lives. Leaving Charleston that last day of ACE and anticipating the fifteen-hour drive ahead, I listened to tape after tape and thought of those many faces. I pull them out once in a while, and remember those two years of teaching in Charleston. Those many faces, memories, and lessons that remind me that, while I was teaching them, they were teaching me as well.

I remained in Catholic education, and my fellow ACE 2 classmate, Tom, and I headed to Bishop Dunne Catholic School in Dallas, Texas. We brought the Three Pillars with us, and looked forward to the challenges, the lessons, and especially the new faces we would encounter. I still recall meeting that first class there, my first class after ACE, and I recall one student who stood out. After the first test I said, "Adarely, you would love Notre Dame." Four years passed by quickly as I taught Adarely in multiple classes, saw her lead various retreats, and even manage the soccer team. Adarely went on to attend Notre Dame, teach as a member of ACE 12, and come full circle to return to teach at Bishop Dunne Catholic School. I remember discussing with fellow ACErs how wonderful it would be to have one of our students follow in our footsteps and become an ACE teacher. Adarely made that dream come true and, on her journey, has inspired countless numbers of her own students to believe in their dreams. Her journey is still developing, and I am excited to see where the next step will lead her.

Coming full circle in building relationships that help me to experience God, I get to tell people that I "met my soul mate in high school." Granted I was in my early thirties at the time, but in the classroom down the hall, I met an art teacher with the same passion for Catholic education, students, and family as I had. My wife, Molly, and I still teach at Bishop Dunne Catholic School today and have the added blessing of having our two daughters, Dani and Delia, come with us each morning to attend the Bishop Dunne Early Childhood Development Center. We look forward to seeing where our journey takes us, and one day I may be sharing stories with one of my daughters as she heads off on her own ACE journey.

These are just a small sample of the memories that ACE has given me. I can sit back and draw on memories that help sustain my passion and remind me what it means to make a difference in the life of someone else and to have them make a difference in your life. Some of the relationships were for the moment, others are long lasting, but all of them allowed me to strengthen my faith. For any one of us, each day brings the opportunity to build new relationships, allowing us to experience God, or allowing others the chance to experience God through us. And I assure you, when someone asks me, "What sustains you in Catholic education?" I have a resounding, if a bit rambling, answer. ✪

Please, Lord:
A Soldier's Experience of Grace

Ryan P. Hinton ACE 11 Savannah

In a soldier's life, an experience of grace is hard to find. This is not only true in combat but also in his or her return from war. A soldier returning from war never has an easy transition, as was the case in my life, but my transition started in an experience of grace through ACE. ACE began for me halfway around the world in Iraq, in the midst of combat and chaos as I searched for information on the program. And my experience of grace came through a senior member of the ACE program.

Sitting on a canvas folding chair in my tent, I looked up at the thermometer and noted the temperature to be 130 degrees. Beads of sweat were forming on my forehead, and I was just sitting there almost motionless. I had just come off of a very difficult mission into the heart of Baghdad, and I felt lost. As I sat there, questions began streaming to the forefront of my mind. What was I doing here? What was I going to do after this war? How was I going to return home? And just who would I be when I returned? With every bead of sweat that dropped to the floor a prayer rose to heaven, "Please, Lord." It is funny that even with my four years of theology training and my years in the Army as a Chaplain Assistant, this simple prayer was all that I could call upon in my time of need. And yet this was the prayer that carried me forward as questions surrounded me.

These questions replayed for weeks; after every mission they were present. I prayed the same simple prayer, "Please, Lord." This prayer was not a plea for mercy from what surrounded me but an invitation for guidance. I was seeking the "burning bush" experience and yet none of bushes in the desert caught the flame of guidance that I was seeking. I expressed my questions to my Chaplain with whom I had worked for several years. I was looking for guidance but instead I received another question. My Chaplain asked, "What were you going to be before you joined the military?" My answer was short and came forth with such clarity it shocked me, "A teacher." He told me to start there and see where it went. Again I prayed, "Please, Lord."

The next morning during my fifteen minutes of personal computer time, instead of my usual update to my parents, I searched the Internet for the ACE Program. I had learned about ACE in my undergraduate years. As the ACE website came up I quickly jotted down any information that I could and tried to e-mail different ACE personnel. Before I knew it, my fifteen minutes were up and I had to wait until the next day. I thought to myself, "Was this going to be the opportunity to return home on my terms? Was this going to serve as my burning bush?" And so I waited praying, "Please, Lord."

The next day I received numerous "undeliverable messages," from the ACE personnel except for one. The only email that had made it through was responded to and the reply came from Joyce Johnstone. This may not have been the burning bush I was looking for, but Joyce did provide me the guidance that I had requested with my simple prayer. She brought me from asking questions about the program to helping me through the application process. I emailed Joyce regularly from that point on; in fact, she was the second phone call that I made upon my return home from Iraq. Joyce became a friend beyond ACE. I would have to say that she was, in fact, the portion of God's grace that I needed at that time to get me through my transition home. Joyce had come through the Vietnam War with a measure of understanding that she offered to me. It was this understanding that provided me with hope when I returned from Iraq.

I eventually had an interview for the program on the campus of Notre Dame. I had flown there from Fort Campbell realizing that I was not assured a place in the program, but knowing that the thought of being a part of the ACE program had provided me with an experience of grace. On my way to meet with Joyce for the first time, I went to what would later become my two favorite places on campus: the Grotto and the God, Country, Notre Dame door of the Basilica. There I prayed, "Please Lord." After I was accepted into the ACE program I returned to those places every day, rain or shine, and continued my prayer. I did

Spirituality

this in recognition of what God had given me through ACE and through the military.

The transition from soldier to teacher began that day and the process continues through this day. My experience of grace was the entirety of the ACE program that began with Joyce but certainly did not end there; rather, it intensified and grew. I am still teaching and have also returned to the military in the Army Reserve, all by the grace of God and with the simple prayer, "Please, Lord." As I rise in the morning, as I tie my tie, when I put on my military uniform, and before I begin every class, I pray, "Please, Lord." ✪

Don't Stop Believing: The Journey of an ACE 11

Laura Giannuzzi ACE 11 Pensacola

Being a double major at Notre Dame in Marketing and Film, Television, and Theater, most people would probably not have thought I would be working in ministry today. Before I arrived at Notre Dame as an undergraduate, I was dead-set on being a television producer. I pursued this path with summer internships in New York at major media outlets. But it was my time studying in Dublin during the spring of my junior year that changed that path. There I met Michael Downs, campus minister for Notre Dame's international programs and an ACE graduate. I also met the post-ACErs who were teaching in Dublin, including Kelly Holohan. All of a sudden my priorities changed quite a bit and before I knew it, I was returning to Notre Dame for my senior year with the intention to a do a post-graduate service program. And thankfully, that program was ACE.

While in ACE, I taught fifth grade in Pensacola, Florida, but I also had an opportunity to teach fourth grade religion. During this time, I realized the students' religion textbook was teaching me more about the faith than anything had before. They say that "you learn when you teach," and this was exactly the case for me. Many of the things I had learned along my faith journey—from the example of my parents, as a child in CCD class, or from high school and college theology courses—these lessons were finally coming together through the very simple explanations given in this children's religion textbook. It was like I was going through RCIA class even though I was already fully initiated into the Catholic Church. And I began to believe that, if I was going to be the Catholic school teacher I wanted to be, I needed to know more about the faith in general. This experience of teaching elementary-level religion during my years in ACE planted within me a desire to study the faith more seriously. I knew if I was going to call myself Catholic, believe in the Church, and teach this as truth to young people, then I needed some better background in my faith and some solid defense for what the Church taught.

In my second year in ACE, I was invited to a study group at a local parish. Their main subject of discussion was the Theology of the Body, Pope John Paul II's reflections on the human person, and I was eager to join. I had not heard of Theology of the Body at this point, but the more the parishioners explained to me, the more intrigued I was. This invitation came at a very important time in my own faith life and in my personal life. I had been somewhat doubting the Church and the faith at the time, even though I was teaching and living that faith every day as best as I could. I previously had some very strong evangelical Christian influences in my life and I was impressed by how "on fire" for Jesus they were and how they lived their lives, from being involved in their church to being so knowledgeable about the Bible. This was particularly evident in the "Bible Belt" where I was teaching; here the Catholic presence was small but the evangelical Christian presence was clearly evident. When it comes down to it, I was really in search of Truth, with a capital "T." The Lord answered my prayers with the Theology of the Body, which deepened my faith life as well as my desire to study theology formally. If there was anything I wanted to study more and teach to others, this was it!

But it wasn't enough to grow in knowledge of my faith; I had to put it into practice. As an ACE teacher, there never seemed to be a shortage of opportunities to serve the school in a variety of ways. Like many ACE teachers, I coached and helped at other school events. By my second year, I was leading the youth choir every Wednesday for school Mass and was helping my principal with our faculty retreat. Some of the best times I had in ACE involved my work in ministry as moderator of the student council. We did food drives, penny wars, and silent auctions for the school and the neighboring areas. My fifth-grade class also volunteered in a nursing home on Fridays after school during the Lenten season. These service learning opportunities were wonderful assets to my students' education, as well as my own. Though I could not see it at the time, a new calling, worlds away from producing television, was beginning to emerge from my service and thirst to learn more about my faith.

I remained at my school after ACE to continue my work and my discernment. During this transitional time in my life, I was continually strengthened by my faith and the support of family and friends as I found myself going deeper and deeper into Catholicism. Part of this discernment included speaking with others about faith and service, and it was at this time that I gained a clearer picture of how much of an impact ACE had on me. I was continually reminded what a great education I had been blessed with during my undergrad years at Notre Dame and what good training I had received in ACE. I began to see my work as an ACE teacher as both unique and special, and I knew that even if I did not remain in teaching, I would continue the mission that I had begun in the classroom.

By the end of my third year of teaching in Catholic schools at the elementary level, I decided to make the move to full-time campus ministry work. I took a job with the Diocese of Rockville Centre, working on college campuses on Long Island. Though I found myself missing teaching, my time in ACE proved to be an excellent training ground for campus ministry. While teaching and working in campus ministry are quite distinct, I found myself "teaching" all the time, through formal events and presentations as well as through simple everyday interactions with students. I was able to start studying theology formally in the beginning of the school year through a Theology of the Body certificate program. What a joy it has been to be able to bring my love for this teaching to the young adults on campus. I started a study group for the diocese that takes place on one of the college campuses and have already witnessed hearts being transformed. I've even found myself back in the classroom, working as a part-time instructor for a local teen abstinence program, and have put my Master's degree to good use acting as a consultant for the program. This new work has included helping to develop the curriculum, writing lesson plans, and helping new instructors with basic elements of classroom management. Though I thought I had formally left the teaching world when I took the job in campus ministry for my diocese, it was such a blessing to be able to use those gifts developed in ACE to help this abstinence program get off the ground.

My personal spiritual journey throughout my time in ACE was such a blessing. From producer to campus minister, from the studio to the classroom to college campuses, my journey has been wrought with many ups and downs, but littered with signs and God's guiding hand along the way. Through the tough times and the great times, I am where I am today because of my faith and because of the fertile soil ACE provided, especially while bonding with such a strong community. From daily Mass in the summer time, to retreats throughout the year, to simple prayers or spiritual discussions—they were all very special, and very formative. Each experience helped me to be a better teacher and becoming the best teacher I could has enabled me to be successful in campus ministry today. I would never be where I am today without ACE and I am eternally grateful for those years of formation. Father Ted Hesburgh said in his recent letter to the Notre Dame family that students come to Notre Dame "to learn how to make best use of their God-given talents and be educated for a life of service." Though my background is varied and my path has had many twists and turns, I believe I have been educated for a life of service, and I hope I can continue to be part of this great Notre Dame tradition.

How I Became a Principal

Tricia Sevilla  ACE 6 Jacksonville
ACE Leadership 6

I believe God sends us signs to direct us on the path of life, and my career in education is a testament to that. If it weren't for ACE, I would not be who I am now. Whenever a fork in the road appeared, God nudged me in the right direction.

That's how I began with the ACE program. John Staud and I spoke not long into the start of my first summer. He knew I had applied for several post-graduate teaching programs, and he was glad I chose ACE over the others. I set him straight; after all, ACE was the only program that accepted me, so I was grateful to him and the other administrators. I won't forget the surprised look on his face and his words, "To be perfectly honest, I'm surprised to hear you say that. I can't say I'm sorry you were turned down because I'm glad you're with us." I saw it as God making sure I followed the right path to shape my life as a teacher.

My foray into the world of education was incredibly difficult and incredibly rewarding, and after five years I felt compelled to see what else the world offered. I joined the corporate world and the land of the bottom line, never quite leaving education behind since I still trained professionals. I didn't know until later that God meant for me to walk down that business path.

As I wandered the travails of life for the next two years, what never left was the pull of the classroom, of being with students and the camaraderie of a faculty and staff. That feeling cannot be duplicated in any type of corporate environment. I prayed that God would help me find my way back to the path I was supposed to follow. God listened.

After Mass one weekend, I picked up the parish bulletin and browsed through it. My eyes caught a corner in which the diocese advertised a search to fill the position of principal for an elementary school. I wondered—could I do that? Just a thought, I shook it off and went about my business. The following Sunday, I picked up the bulletin again and the notice was still there. I have to admit, the thought sat in the back of my mind all week. Would Pat Tierney, our superintendent, think I was crazy for even thinking of applying for this job? I said to myself, if it's still there next week I'll take it as a sign.

Throughout the week I constantly questioned if I even had the skill set to be a principal. I reasoned that I was a solid teacher, had a Master's degree, and my experience working in the executive office and store of a corporate business gave me insight to the management and financial aspects required for the job. I can do it, I thought to myself, I can do it! Lo and behold, that Sunday the bulletin still held the same message.

But I didn't call Pat right away. I needed to go up to Notre Dame and represent our local alumni club at the Alumni Senate. I saw it as a chance to evaluate my situation thoroughly before jumping off the deep end and switching careers again. God saw it as a way to remind me that I needed to pay attention.

The first Alumni Senate event was a dinner honoring the recipient of the Distinguished Young Alumni Award. I couldn't believe who I saw: Benny Morton of my ACE cohort, currently a principal of a couple of years. Wow, I thought, if he can do it, why can't I?

The next evening's keynote speaker was Lou Nanni whose impassioned question to the alumni was this: "Notre Dame has given you an education. How have you given it back?" I felt Lou's eyes bore into my soul and make me wonder about my career choice. When I was a teacher I gave back my time, my talent, my treasure. What was I doing now?

Everywhere I turned, God posted signs for me: the bulletin notice, seeing Benny, Lou Nanni. His message was becoming impossible to ignore. There was only one thing left to do—meet with Pat Tierney. I was determined; the minute I returned to Jacksonville, I would call her and ask her about being a principal, no matter how crazy she thought I was!

Once the senate forum ended, I toyed between catching the early or late bus back to Chicago. I walked to LaFortune Student Center to wait, and when I came out I ran into the friendly ACE face of John Staud. Greeting me, he said that he heard I left the education world and wondered what I was up to these days. Not quite ready to say my crazy idea aloud, I confided I was thinking about returning, but it was dependent on a conversation with Pat Tierney. He casually looked at me and said, "Oh, she's upstairs." I didn't think I heard him right, "What do you mean she's upstairs?"

As it turns out, this was the opening retreat weekend where all new ACErs meet each other and their administrators. I couldn't believe it. The one person from Jacksonville that I needed to speak to was here at Notre Dame doing an ACE-related event! This was God putting up the neon-lights-on-Broadway-highway-billboard sign saying, "Follow Me."

Needless to say, I took the later bus. Pat and I talked for a while, discussed my credentials, and her last words to me that afternoon were, "The minute you get back to Jacksonville, email your cover letter and resume to the pastor. Here's his address."

I'm now in the midst of my second year as principal of Resurrection Catholic School and am a member of ACE Leadership 6. I was ACE 6, now I'm ALP 6. I think God meant for me to be here.

This Is Not What I Signed Up For

Nick Huck  ACE 11 Atlanta

There aren't too many things in life that I knew I was meant to do, but ACE was one of them.

My admissions interview went well and I somehow knew I should say "yes" to ACE if they said "yes" to me. That said, waiting for ACE's reply filled me with the nervousness of a new teacher's first day of school. Rejection meant not only pouring a substantial amount of time and effort onto infertile soil, but also realizing I was obviously wrong about the only thing I ever thought I was right about. Thankfully, I was accepted and signed up for ACE.

I signed up for ACE expecting to change students' academic careers and coach great teams. I thought community prayer night was a given. While I knew there would be challenges, I didn't think these challenges would be any greater than my physics or chemistry course in college.

But as the months in ACE wore on, I began to see that ACE wasn't exactly what I expected. I realized I did not receive what I signed up for.

I didn't sign up to coach "wrassling." In Georgia, "wrassling" is the sport where boys try to pin each other. "Wrestling" is the sport where you tackle steer. The athletic director asked—no, told me—that I would coach wrassling. I balked since I had never even attended a wrestling match, but no argument would win over the athletic director.

I didn't sign up to help teach pole vault in track or coach girls' junior varsity volleyball. My experience at basketball and distance running didn't prepare me well for these sports. I balked, again unsuccessfully, at pole vault and realized later there was no point in balking at junior varsity volleyball.

I didn't sign up for driving thirty miles each way to school which meant sometimes spending two hours in the car moving through Atlanta traffic.

I didn't sign up to have students circulate cruel and vicious rumors about me.

I didn't sign up for living as individuals in a house until January when relationships finally were forged into community.

I didn't sign up to prepare four different course preps, one of which was the first time the school offered the course, while writing a curriculum for the course, and needing to turn in such detailed lesson plans, that they would have put Doc Doyle's to shame.

I wasn't the only one who did not get what they signed up for. Several other friends were challenged to say yes in trying situations. ACErs like Tina, who lesson planned for five different classes and taught two classes simultaneously at the same time in the same room. Karl floated between five different classrooms on two floors in two different buildings. Those are two of those who said yes and didn't get what they signed up for.

There's another girl I heard of who didn't get what she signed up for. As a teenager she said yes to bearing God's Son. She didn't sign up for having Simeon at the Temple steps prophesize that a sword would pierce her heart. She didn't sign up for people plotting her Son's death. She didn't sign up for false accusations and stories to be spread about her Son. She didn't sign up to learn her Son narrowly escaped a crowd who wanted to stone him to death. She didn't sign up to witness her Son's murder.

Yet her yes brought about salvation. Perhaps my yes participated in that same salvation. Her yes was unconditional. My yes was sometimes cheerful and willing and was at other times tired, sporadic, and cynical. While she said yes to everything, I said no to chaperoning Prom, a weekend retreat, and numerous other requests. Her example of pouring herself unconditionally into God's request reminded me what my yes was—often conditional and set upon my own terms. Mary's example also reminded me of what I should become.

Without Mary's yes there would be no salvation. Without my yes, Thomas wouldn't have earned fifth at the State Wrassling Meet. The girls' volleyball team might not have won more than fifty percent of its games and enjoyed a fantastic season. Tim might still be wondering if his pole vault steps were correct. Without my yes, Erin, who shared the drive with me, and I would not have developed a friendship to the extent of understanding each other with only a glance. Without my yes, my student, Will, and I wouldn't have discussed implications of *The Screwtape Letters* in his life, and Allison wouldn't have seen the death penalty from a prisoner's eyes. Without my yes, the Atlanta ACE community might not have instituted "Mandatory Fun Nights" just so we would make more time to hang out together. Tina's students learned about adapting to pressures through her example, and Karl's students saw his great Christian witness.

Mary's yes brought hope for the world. My yes and the multitude of ACErs' responses of yes brought about and continue to bring hope to students and to each other. ☘

APPENDIX

Appendix

Cast Your Nets Deeper: Celebrating 10 Years of ACE

Keynote Address: Rev. Tim Scully, C.S.C.
Saturday, July 26, 2003

One day as Jesus was standing by the Lake of Gennesaret, with the people crowding around him and listening to the word of God, he saw at the water's edge two boats, left there by the fishermen, who were washing their nets. He got into one of the boats, the one belonging to Simon, and asked him to put out a little from shore. Then he sat down and taught the people from the boat. When he had finished speaking, he said to Simon, "Put out into deep water, and let down the nets for a catch." Simon answered, "Master, we've worked hard all night and haven't caught anything. But because you say so, I will let down the nets." When they had done so, they caught such a large number of fish that their nets began to break. So they signaled their partners in the other boat to come and help them, and they came and filled both boats so full that they began to sink. When Simon Peter saw this, he fell at Jesus' knees and said, "Go away from me, Lord; I am a sinful man!" For he and all his companions were astonished at the catch of fish they had taken, and so were James and John, the sons of Zebedee, Simon's partners. Then Jesus said to Simon, "Don't be afraid; from now on you will catch people." So they pulled their boats up on shore, left everything and followed him. (A retelling of Luke 5:1-11)

What an extraordinary story to mark this occasion. Luke offers a great passage for this moment in which we find ourselves—this moment in ACE's growth, this moment in the history of Catholic education in this country, this moment in our larger Church's history, and perhaps for many of us (certainly for me), this moment in our own lives. Because the central motivation in this passage, what makes this whole passage unfold, is this one simple, specific command by Christ, "Go deeper." Put out into deeper water. "Cast your nets deeper." The Spirit of the ever-restless Christ Teacher, on whom we have come to rely since ACE's inception, is at it again! Never content to let his disciples rest in the familiar, in what they already know, in what they have already accomplished, Christ Teacher, with a restless, inspired vision, urges us in ACE onward—into the unknown, into the deep, into the as yet unimagined.

Jesus, of course, utters these words to the unlikeliest of people—his beleaguered disciples—hungry and overwhelmed fishermen sitting ashore by empty nets after a long and fruitless night's work. Simon, exhausted and skeptical, reminds him that they have fished—hard—all night, but have caught nothing. He's dispirited. And yet, at the same time, you almost get the sense that Peter has come to know his friend Jesus well enough that, buried beneath his protest ("We've been working all night but have caught nothing."), there exists an almost resigned hope in this Jesus, who finds the most unlikely, imaginative routes out of seemingly dead-end situations—a hope that He might transform this situation yet again. It's as though Peter is saying, "I saw what you did with the crowd of 5,000. With the man born blind. The leper. Well, it's been one long night on the lake, and we are all hungry...who knows...?"

At this point in their friendship, Peter must have hardly been surprised that Jesus, immediately, invites him to climb back into the boat, back onto Lake Gennesaret, the scene of Peter's latest failure, to go fishing again. But notice, this will be no free ride for Peter and the disciples—no flying fish jumping into his net while they sit back and nap. Instead, as always, there is an invitation, a command even, to get back to work, with a deeper faith; back to the mission, with more trusting belief.

"Put out into deeper waters! You see, you caught nothing last night because you fished in those same shallow, familiar waters! I know that spot worked for you yesterday—and the day before, and the day before. But the same old practices don't always work!" It's as though Jesus is enticing Peter, trying to light a fire in him, challenging the disciples, "Where is your imagination? Your boldness? Where has your vision gone? Have I accomplished all these good things before just so you could start thinking small? Now, put out into deeper, unfamiliar waters. And be not afraid. Have faith in me. I will come with you. I will show you the way."

"Dream boldly," Jesus dares us. "There is more life in this lake than you can imagine!"

I just love this passage. It reveals the boundless imagination Christ Teacher had for his disciples, and for their mission. Perhaps this passage speaks to those of us in Catholic education, and for us in ACE, and in the broader Church, in a particular way this afternoon. The disciples, like us in ACE, have experienced some not-inconsequential initial successes with this enigmatic preacher and miracle-worker Jesus. Even at times, they have been awestruck, amazed at what Jesus has accomplished, often with and through them. There have been periodic eruptions of a strange new power in their midst. Surely, their hearts are filled with gratitude for this new energy, this unforeseen passion and new direction that has refocused their lives, giving their days a fresh and deep meaning, their lives trajectory that excites and fulfills them.

And yet, some days, like this one on the lakeside, empty nets beside them, tired and spent, the magic seems lost in routine. So much work, so much energy expended, and yet the needs remain unfulfilled.

And so they find themselves encountering the person who got them involved in this crazy life in the first place. Again and again, throughout their lives, the disciples return to Jesus—Christ Teacher—for direction.

But why look for new life? Why turn to Jesus in search of a new challenge? There's one sense in which the only thing to do on this great tenth anniversary weekend is just to give thanks. We give thanks for the wild, wonderful explosion of charism and energy, vision and vocation that the Holy Spirit has unleashed in ACE over the years. We give thanks for how the Holy Spirit has called each of us, now 694 ACE teachers strong, to give our lives, in some way, to children and to Catholic education. We rejoice in that and just give thanks. Look at the faces gathered here today: the gifts, the generosity, the charisma, the friendships, the marriages, the religious vocations, the deep faith.

And yet, dare I say it, the hunger in this room, the still untapped potential, the thirst for more, the restless hearts. Those hundreds of you still planted firmly in the midst of classrooms and schools around the country, as well as those who are living out vocations outside the classroom, know so tangibly how much work there is to do. In one sense, we realize how little ACE has accomplished in the face of the needs that are out there. You have felt (haven't you?) from time to time, the exasperation of Peter and the disciples, sitting by near-empty nets, hungry and out of gas. You've felt that fatigue at the three o'clock bell after a long day of teaching, or grading tests that are stacked too high. Or counseling a student who's going through more than seems imaginable. Or watching a school struggle for new sources of enthusiasm and mission, or trying to hold on to its Catholic character. A diocese trying to figure out how to keep its inner-city schools afloat. Or looking for meaning or consistency in your personal, professional, or spiritual life. Or a friend to pray and share life with at a deep level.

In the face of such need, of such opportunity, do we dare, with Peter and the first disciples, to turn to our mysterious, adventurous teacher, who got us involved in this madness to begin with? Do we dare to protest, justly protest, about all that remains to be done, despite our efforts? And do so knowing that buried in our protest is a hope-filled challenge to Christ Teacher to show us another miracle? And that, if he finds our hearts believing, he will show us the way. And yet, if the Gospels teach us anything about Jesus, miracles won't be magic, instantaneous, and painless cure-alls, with nothing demanded of us, no sacrifice, no hard work, no imagination. This wasn't the case with the first 10 years of ACE, and it won't be now. It will be rather what Christ's miracles always are—an invitation to us to respond, to cast our nets deeper, to imagine unexplored possibilities, and to go forth, one step at a time, and make the unimagined a reality.

If there exists one single danger when one worships, as we do, in a Church as wonderfully ancient and institutionalized as ours, it is perhaps that we might not always be the first to imagine what is possible. Perhaps the greatest danger in our own ecclesial context is a failure to imagine new life and possibility in the midst of what seem insurmountable obstacles and limitations. How can these empty nets possibly get filled? How can we serve the Gospel more effectively, given the challenges—and opportunities—that confront contemporary Catholicism in America? How can we serve our schools and our children better?

Look at the storied beginning of the Catholic school system in the United States. An immigrant minority, mostly poor and ignorant, a cultural and linguistic mosaic of peoples from every part of the "old world," fleeing their circumstances, arriving in this land during the mid- and late nineteenth, and early twentieth centuries, searching for freedom and opportunity. They were, in large part, immigrants from Catholic countries, and they were greeted by the dominant culture with deep suspicion and hostility. In part because our forebearers were Catholic and foreign, and therefore "un-American," they were largely excluded from the cultural and social institutions that defined American life and society. American "common" schools were—from their founding—permeated by secular values, practices, and attitudes, couched in White Protestant ideology, and not so subtly engaged in promoting the notion that Catholicism was inimical to Americanism.

It was into this exceptionally hostile cultural, social, and political reality that a courageous band of women and men, at the time largely vowed women, brought a vision for a vast network of schools that would serve to nourish and strengthen Catholic culture and identity in this new, and often openly unwelcoming, context. And beginning with Elizabeth Ann Seton, Katharine Drexel, and John Neumann, these women and men gave their lives to build what would become the world's largest private school system. These women and men built over 10,000 schools across America, and at one point were educating over twelve percent of the American school population! There is nothing in the world organizationally like the American Catholic school system; it is the product of the imagination, the risk-taking, and the sacrifice of our forbearers in the faith.

Now, if I may, a couple of things are abundantly clear in our contemporary context:

1. Catholic schools have never been more important than they are today. Today, these schools continue to play the role that they have played historically of preserving and deepening the identity of our Church in contemporary America, a land today less anti-Catholic, but certainly even more seductively secular and materialistic.

2. After preparing generations of immigrant American Catholics for fuller participation in American culture and society, in some senses these schools have become victims of their own success, resulting in greater prosperity for some sectors of the American Catholic population, and a related diminished interest in preserving and maintaining a distinctively faith-based educational alternative.

3. Today, these fragile schools are often serving school populations in areas of our cities and towns that are underserved and deeply needy. They sometimes represent the only escape children have from cycles of poverty and hopelessness to which they have been condemned. Like the immigrants of the previous two centuries, Catholic schools represent a ray of hope in a country, a city, a system that seems to be offering little hope.

4. The Holy Spirit has sent us a message that the present and future vitality of these schools rests in the hands of the laity, and the biggest challenge we face is providing committed leaders for the now 8,500 Catholic elementary and high schools that stretch across this land.

ACE is, in a most powerful way, a collective act of faith-filled imagination. It is a "casting the nets more deeply" every day. It rests on the constant, evolving, generous risk-taking, sacrifice, and imagination of a collection of disciples, the almost 700 ACErs now who have joined our movement on behalf of spreading the Gospel through Catholic education. ACE relies on your daily "Yes!" to the challenges before us—the "Yes" you shared the day you entered the movement and the countless "Yes's" you have made since that day. I believe that Christ Teacher, through the inspiration of the Holy Spirit, has more—much more—for us to do. And it's going to take bold imagination and courageous response on our part.

Today, perhaps more than ever before, our times call for dreaming new dreams for our schools and our children, for "wishful thinking" and "thoughtful wishing." We need to imagine new possibilities to, as Thomas More said it, "serve God in the tangle of our minds." You may remember the scene in Robert Bolt's play, *A Man for All Seasons*. Thomas explains to his daughter, Margaret, why he is taking the difficult and dangerous position he does in opposition to the king. When she objects to this stubborn and painful path, he tells her, "God made the angels to show Him splendor, as He made animals for innocence and plants for their simplicity. But man He made to serve Him wittily in the tangle of his mind!"

That is, it seems to me, precisely right! So, where is our imagination, where is our mind—inspired by faith and unafraid of failure, and restless for challenge—leading ACE as we move forward?

Without being self-congratulatory, but recognizing what the Holy Spirit has put together here, we need to realize the unique opportunity that we in the ACE community have because of the foundation that the Holy Spirit has built, with our cooperation, over the past ten years. Over seventy percent of our 500 ACE graduates have decided to remain in education, the majority in Catholic education. ACE now prepares more Catholic educators than any college or university in the nation by a long shot! The quality of the ACE teachers, the quality of their education, and the quality of their experience is stronger than ever, thanks in great part to the extraordinary dedication and commitment of Doc Doyle, Joyce Johnstone, and John Staud and the ACE faculty and staff. Each year we are serving increasing numbers of disadvantaged students, with an increasing focus on traditionally undereducated minority groups. The faculty being assembled here is fast becoming one of the premier teacher education faculties in the country.

We can put together the resources to dream boldly about the future of Catholic education. Already, ACE has begun to branch out in imaginative ways consistent with our core mission. The ACE South Bend Program now allows career-changers to become ACE teachers. ACE South Bend teachers now teach in six of the eight grades at St. Adalbert's, which serves one of the most diverse and disadvantaged populations in South Bend. Not only is St. Adalbert's being revitalized, but ACE will be able to research our results there as a model case for school-wide effects of the ACE Program.

Through ACE's Office of Educational Outreach, fourteen partnering programs are now up and running from coast to coast, following the ACE model, providing over 200 more teachers annually to 160 more schools. This year alone, together we are providing 400 wonderfully educated and talented teachers to nearly 30,000 school children across America!

The ACE Leadership Program, led by Fr. Ron Nuzzi, is currently educating 20 ACE graduates and other career teachers to assume leadership in Catholic schools. And this effort is only going to grow. We have brought to Notre Dame the research capacity, with added resources through the Institute for Educational Initiatives, to identify and promulgate best practices from our own, and others', experiences. *Catholic Education: A Journal of Inquiry and Practice* is now housed at, and funded by, Notre Dame, and serves as another example of how we are trying to follow the lead of the Spirit in service to our mission of evangelizing through Catholic education.

But this is only the beginning. In particular, as many of you have expressed to me and the ACE staff over the past several years, it is crucial to recognize—because it's so blatantly obvious to anyone who looks around this room—that we have only just begun to tap the collective potential among the growing ACE and post-ACE communities. It is critical that we think this through boldly with all of our faith, will and imagination to cast our nets deeper! There is just too much outright giftedness in our extended ACE community, and too much need outside this room, in our Catholic schools, not to follow wherever the Holy Spirit is leading us.

I'd like to suggest a couple things, and just as importantly, I'd like to begin a conversation here talking among ourselves, about the future. But first, let me share some preliminary thoughts about two ideas that we have been praying and thinking about here at Notre Dame.

First, ACE graduates interested in continuing in Catholic schools have identified three challenges to us over the last seven years: 1) low salaries (no surprise there!); 2) the lack of opportunity for professional development and advancement; and 3) an underdeveloped sense of faith community among one's peers.

As at least a partial response, we would like to commence in the coming year an ACE Fellows Initiative. ACE Fellows will bring together a core group of selected ACE graduates to make a deeper commitment to provide imaginative, effective solutions to the problems facing needy K-12 schools. ACE graduates will be invited to submit creative initiatives in response to these, or other, areas of need that we identify. ACE Fellows will be encouraged to work, together and apart, to form a thoughtful community in service to Catholic education. We look to provide modest annual stipends not only to help supplement teacher incomes, but to incentivize innovative and successful initiatives focused on the improvement of Catholic education. Fellows will be appointed for a multi-year period, in which part of their commitment would entail convening 2-3 times a year (perhaps once at Notre Dame during the ACE summer, and 1-2 regional retreats during the year), to discuss issues, share strategies, develop long-term initiatives for school improvement, and to pray and share fellowship together.

A second dimension I'd at least like to begin dialoguing about this weekend stems from the late John Cardinal O'Connor's visit to the ACE Program five years ago to celebrate the ACE Missioning Mass. At his invitation, I met with Cardinal O'Connor in New York City later that year, and as I was giving him an update on our hopes for the ACE Program, he finally stopped me and said, "Look, Tim, the ACE Program is wonderful. But from what I witnessed that weekend, I honestly think you're thinking too small. ACE is more than a two-year service program. It's a movement—a lay apostolic movement in service to Catholic education."

Now, for whatever reason, that conversation has never left me. On the one hand, that's a slightly intimidating phrase—"lay apostolic movement." But I suppose part of the point is, "Who knows exactly what it means?" That's up for the Holy Spirit, using each of us, to inspire!

I spoke earlier about how the Catholic Church in this country, and the Catholic school system, really grew up and flourished in immigrant communities. The rich devotions that were cultivated during that time—the rosary, the Stations of the Cross, Adoration, Corpus Christi processions down Main Street—all grew out of the needs and hopes of a hungry, immigrant population. And I guess there's a sense in which many of us understood how to be Catholic in this way, as immigrants, if you will. But there's one problem: many of us are not really immigrants any more. Now, some among us are even affluent (relative to our grandparents), educated, culturally mainstream, more mobile and geographically disparate—and many are struggling for meaningful ways to live out our Catholic identity. There's a sense in which the old, immigrant Catholicism set in the context of a hostile land doesn't quite fit many of us anymore, but we're not sure what the alternatives are. Maybe because there don't exist many meaningful alternatives at this point. Faith communities seem to thrive in pilgrim settings in a way they haven't yet achieved in a more mainstream setting. This was certainly the case in this country. So the question becomes, "How are we being called to live out our faith amidst the affluence and secularism and sophistication of our modern American culture?"

Of course, as far as the spiritual life and the apostolic life are concerned, we're all still immigrants, still journeying towards a home, still searching for deeper authenticity, still hungering and hoping. We can't lose sight of that, because that hunger, that searching, keeps drawing us back to Christ. How do we nurture that spiritual hunger and that apostolic fervor today?

In the end, the best path may be our collective response to try to find ways to live holy lives in our Church, in service to Catholic education, within the lived realities of our lives—married, single, religious, in vibrant parishes, in not-so-vibrant parishes, living alone, living in community, scattered across every state in the nation and beyond. And yet, across all those differences and ways of life, we have been called together. We've been called to serve Catholic schools at this absolutely critical time. And, in large part because we've said an initial "Yes" to that, we've been called to imagine new and truly meaningful ways of nurturing that vocation.

"Put out into deeper waters, and let down the nets for a catch," the Teacher invites and admonishes us. Let's dream together, dreams worthy of the extraordinary institutional legacy we have inherited. And as we do, we can trust that Jesus will lead us to new, and previously unimagined, possibilities.

Appendix

ACE FACTS

996 teachers have served in Catholic schools through the ACE program since 1994.

40 teachers were in ACE 1 and 90 teachers are in ACE 15.

ACE 1 served 8 dioceses and the program now serves 27 dioceses.

100 Catholic school principals have gone through the ACE Leadership Program since 2002.

The ACE Leadership program serves 47 dioceses across the country.

32 teachers have been in the English as a New Language (ENL) program in the first 2 cohorts.

20 communities in cities across the country are part of the ACE Fellowship.

15 programs participate in the University Consortium for Catholic Education (UCCE).

Over 475 teachers serve every year in Catholic schools through the UCCE.

Over 1,500 teachers have participated in UCCE programs since 1994.

Over 75% of ACE graduates remain professionally involved in the field of education.

Over 50% of ACE graduates teach in classrooms or lead schools as administrators.

Of the group that remains in schools, over 75% serve in Catholic schools.

Over a dozen students taught by ACE teachers went on to become ACE teachers.

Approximately 25% of ACE alumni are seeking or hold additional graduate degrees.

4 ACE alumni have pursued the priesthood or religious life.

Over 100 ACE alumni married someone from ACE.

About the Editors

Laura (Considine) Budzichowski graduated from Notre Dame with a B.A. in Psychology and minor in Spanish. She was a member of ACE 2 and taught Spanish at Resurrection Catholic School in Pascagoula, Mississippi. After ACE, Laura moved to Detroit, Michigan, where she worked with a venture capital firm before attending law school at the University of Michigan. After graduating from law school, Laura and her husband, Zack, moved to Charlotte, North Carolina, where Laura practices corporate law, with a focus on mergers and acquisitions.

Zack Budzichowski received a B.S. in Mechanical Engineering from Notre Dame. He was a member of ACE 2 and taught high school math, science, and computers at Resurrection Catholic School in Pascagoula, Mississippi. After ACE, Zack moved to Detroit, Michigan, where he embarked on a five-year career in automotive engineering. Zack and his wife, Laura, currently reside in Charlotte, North Carolina, where Zack is a stay-at-home parent.

Tony DeSapio studied Economics and Political Science at Notre Dame. He was in ACE 6 and taught third grade at St. Paul Catholic School in Memphis, Tennessee. For the past seven years, he has served on the ACE Staff working in Educational Outreach, and in 2004, founded the ACE Fellowship as an effort to build a national movement in service to Catholic education. His work with the ACE Fellowship keeps him actively engaged with the community of nearly 1,000 ACE graduates as well as a broad base of other advocates for Catholic schools.

K.C. Kenney received his degree as a student in the Program of Liberal Studies department at the University of Notre Dame. During his two years of service as a part of ACE 12, K.C. taught language arts, religion, and social studies to the seventh and eighth graders of St. Vincent de Paul Catholic School in Mobile, Alabama. Upon completing his time with ACE, K.C.'s love of learning and desire to continue service pointed him in the direction of medical school. He is currently finishing the prerequisite coursework necessary to take the MCAT at The Ohio State University and hopes to start medical school in 2010.

Kathy Steinlage graduated from St. Mary's College with a double B.A. in Psychology and Humanistic Studies, as well as a minor in Music. Following her graduation, Kathy joined ACE 7 and taught middle school literature and religion in Mission, Texas, at Our Lady of Sorrows School. She stayed a third year in the Rio Grande Valley before moving to Santiago, Chile, where she taught with the ChACE program at St. George's College. Following her South American adventure, Kathy returned to the United States and moved to Los Angeles, where she taught at St. Sebastian School. For the past two years, Kathy has worked as Assistant Director of the ACE Fellowship, and has enjoyed traveling across the country and visiting with ACE alumni and supporters of Catholic education. She plans to return to the classroom next year and will be moving to Denver, Colorado.

www.ingramcontent.com/pod-product-compliance
Lightning Source LLC
Chambersburg PA
CBHW060740050426
42449CB00008B/1277